Worry and be Happy

The Audacity of Hopelessness

Karl Renz

Worry and be Happy

The Audacity of Hopelessness

Karl Renz

Edited By
Manjit Achhra

You came and you will be gone.
You don't even have to do something for it, it happens by itself.
You came by itself and you will be gone by itself.
So, what do you worry about?

Karl Renz

Worry and be Happy

Copyright © 2013 Karl Renz

First Edition: January 2013

PUBLISHED BY
ZEN PUBLICATIONS
60, Juhu Supreme Shopping Centre,
Gulmohar Cross Road No. 9, JVPD Scheme,
Juhu, Mumbai 400 049. India.
Tel: +91 22 32408074
eMail: info@zenpublications.com
Website: www.zenpublications.com

Book Design: Red Sky Designs, Mumbai
Cover Image: Detail of a painting by Karl Renz

ISBN   978-93-82788-04-1

All rights reserved. No part of this book may be reproduced or transmitted in any form or by any means, electronic or mechanical, including photocopying, recording, or by any information storage and retrieval system without written permission from the author or his agents, except for the inclusion of brief quotations in a review.

Contents

YOU ONLY SUFFER BECAUSE YOU HOPE THAT ONE DAY IT WILL BE GOOD	10
YOU PRETEND TO BE SOMEONE AND I'M TOO LAZY TO PRETEND - THAT'S ALL	41
YOU CANNOT BE BURNT DOWN BY YOUR OWN FIRE - BUT YOU TRY	72
MAY IT BE AS IT IS - THAT IS INSTANT FULFILLMENT	106
THERE IS ENLIGHTENMENT - BUT ONLY FOR PHANTOMS	136
CONSCIOUSNESS WANTS NOTHING FROM YOU, IT'S JUST HAVING FUN	164
THERE'S NO HAPPINESS IN ANYTHING ...AND THAT'S THE HAPPY NEWS	189

Other Books by Karl Renz

- A Little Bit Of Nothingness
  81 Observations On The Unnamable
- The Song of Irrelevance
  Meditation of what you are
- Heaven and Hell
- Am I - I Am
- May It Be As It Is
  The Embrace of Helplessness
- If You Wake Up, Don't Take It Personally
  Dialogues in the Presence of Arunachala
- The Myth of Enlightenment
  Seeing Through the Illusion of Separation

Other Books by Zen Publications
- Redemption Stories: Unwasted Pain
- A Duet of One
- Pursue 'Happiness' And Get Enlightened
- Pointers From Ramana Maharshi
- Enlightened Living
- A Buddha's Babble
- A Personal Religion Of Your Own
- The Essence of The Ashtavakra Gita
- The Relationship Between 'I' And 'Me'
- Seeking Enlightenment – Why ?
- Nuggets of Wisdom
- Confusion No More
- Guru Pournima
- Advaita and the Buddha
- It So Happened That... The Unique Teaching of Ramesh S. Balsekar
- Sin and Guilt: Monstrosity of Mind
- The Infamous Ego
- Who Cares?!
- The Essence of the Bhagavad Gita
- Your Head in the Tiger's Mouth
- Consciousness Writes
- Consciousness Speaks
- The Bhagavad Gita – A Selection

ACKNOWLEDGEMENT

The Publishers wish to thank
Sanjay Inamdar, Hemant Nadkarni and Amrita Hinduja
for their invaluable help in making this book possible.

You only suffer because you hope that one day it will be good

Q: Lately I have been told by my friends that this what I want to reach, cannot be reached without a master…

K: Who told you that?

Q: My friends…

K: I would forget them, they sound more like enemies. [Laughter]

Q: But they think I'm lost…

K: Yeah. You are lost. You still have friends?

Q: Yeah…

K: We will work on it. [Laughter]

Q: They take good care of me…

K: That's the problem with friends.

Q: Not all friends take good care…

K: But they always take something – even care [Laughter]. So, what do they say?

Q: They say that the spiritual path, you can't take on your own, somebody has to take you by your hand…

K: Okay. And? [Laughter] First we have to talk about what is your goal, what do you want to reach? Then we can decide if you need

a master or not?

I cannot say yes or no. If your goal is to have a more open view of the world or wider consciousness or become more aware or whatever you call as a spiritual goal, then I would agree that maybe you need some help. But whatever you long for – that what is your nature – no!

Q: For that we don't need help?

K: No. So, yes you need help if your goal is like having an idea of enlightenment then you need a master. If your idea is to become more aware or realize yourself as prior to everything or realize yourself as a spirit or realize yourself as a space, all for whatever you can have a goal – like an idea of a better place, or better circumstance or no-circumstance, whatever you can come-up with, then I agree that you need someone who takes you there.

But to become That what-you-cannot-not-be – That what is your nature – there's no master who can help you. So, yes and no. That's why I asked what's your goal. If you want to be happy, then you have masters for that – who can make you work forever for your bloody happiness. If you need an open heart, then you have many heart masters – surgeons. That we can talk about.

But for That absolute satisfaction what never needs to be satisfied, there's no master, no teacher, nothing to learn. But for all the rest, you can do something. So, you have to decide – maybe – or maybe-not.

Q: Maybe it's not my decision?

K: That's still one too many who has no decision. This excuse we don't buy anymore. No one else can be what-you-are, other than you. So, whose decision would it be? If you think it's not your decision, there's still a decision to make. So, you're already in a wrong idea that something has to be decided. If you cannot decide, grace should decide or God should decide. No! They are more helpless than you. There is no grace for you. No one will ever help you in that.

But for all the rest, for sure there are dream masters and dream goals or dream ways, something to reach. Again, it's always a paradox – yes and no. And I'm just too lazy for all the relative goals. I would rather watch television. That's my relative goal – never to move away from the television. [Laughter]

Q [Laughing]: You reached it...

K: [Laughing] And now we took it away from you. No you cannot get away from the television because you are the Absolute viewer and all this is tell-lie-vision. You never moved, you are the Absolute eye of God who is the Absolute observer – the one and only spectator.

Q [Another visitor]: After meeting many teachers, I met you in Madrid. And I think I missed what you mean by true nature. You are speaking about something that I cannot get...

K: That's your true nature – that what you can't get.

Q: But when you speak about your true nature...

K: No. It's not your 'true' nature, it's nature. 'True' nature is already artificial.

Q: What do you mean by nature?

K: It means That what-you-cannot-not-be which is in the presence and absence of anything you can experience, which is in the presence and in the absence of any experiencer what-you-are. That what never demands anything, that what never needs anything, there is no necessity for what-you-are in anything.

Q: There is no need of Self to realize itself?

K: No need. The Self doesn't need to realize the Self because the Self is Reality permanently realizing itself. It cannot get more realized than it already is. There is no 'more' realization of the Self. Only in the relative dream, there is more or less or gaining something. But not in That what is not a dream.

Q: The nature is the Self?

K: It's called *Sat* and *Sat* is satisfaction – absolute satisfaction, uninterrupted satisfaction. The absolute absence of any idea of existence, and how existence has to be, and could be, and shall be. All those ideas depend on a dream character. The dream character is a phantom and it has all the ideas of masters and servants and slavery – ideas of how it has to be.

But That what-you-are in nature, has absolutely no idea about itself or anything else. So, your nature would say, it's absolute absence of any presence of any idea of what-you-are and what-you-are-not – the absolute absence of any presence of whatever you can imagine. So, you are not an image. But the moment you try to imagine yourself, you become an image of yourself – like a shadow and when you are the shadow of yourself, you miss yourself – that's called suffering, and longing.

So, you suffer out of bullshit – that you found yourself – that's the misery. It's unavoidable. The moment you found yourself, you know yourself, you suffer – anything. That what-you-are cannot be known by itself but when what-you-are knows itself as a person that is born, any idea, any experience – already there's misery.

Q: The absence is also of the Self?

K: Yes. The Self doesn't need any Self, the Self doesn't know any Self. So, for the Self, even the word Self is too much. You could say God doesn't know any God, it doesn't need to know God. But the moment God knows God, there are two Gods – two Gods too many. And then the whole story starts, in the hell of missing – this passionate story of seeking what was never lost. That's called the drama of God in divine comedy, but it's a joke. He's suffering about a joke that he told himself. But now he believes in the joke. Already God is a joke. So, what to do?

We are already finished today. [Laughter]

Q [Another visitor]: I suffered a torment of indecision for last few weeks...

K: That's good. [Laughter]

Q: To me it was so painful, this torment of indecision...

K: Yeah. The schizophrenic yes and no. But sometimes you cannot avoid it. No way out. It's like a divided mind, that's the nature of hell.

Q: Can we do nothing about that?

K: Whatever you do feeds in the fire. You cannot do anything. Even by sitting idle, somewhere trying not to do it, you burn. If the energy is in action and you have to experience yourself as someone who is undecided, you have to experience yourself as that. For what-you-are, there's nothing wrong with it because it's just another energetic event like the next sip of coffee. So, what-you-are is always very cool, absolutely cool, never burns. It just experiences a burning 'me'. And 'me' by nature is misery, you know that.

Q: So, it's just that I'm identified with 'me' that it's burning?

K: No. It's two already – 'me' identifying with 'me'. What-you-are doesn't identify with anything – never. You just experience yourself as the next experience of hell. You cannot escape it because you realize yourself as a 'me' in that drama of being undecided. So, your nature is helplessness but it's still very 'cool'. And there's nothing to gain or lose if it's different. What-you-are has no taste, it would not say this is good or that is bad. It has no idea about good and bad. It just happens.

Q: I just want to have a decision of 'Yes' or 'No'!

K: And then came 'Yes' at the end. [Laughter] Maybe you had to sit here in this dilemma, that all what happened before had to happen exactly as it happened. So, you now being here, questioning the question, demands the past to be as it was. The future demanded the past. All the 'yes' and 'no' had to happen so that now this question could happen.

The totality demands now to be as it is so that future can be, as it already is. And there is no decision to make. It's already decided.

Otherwise why should I sit here? If I had this question – Should I go or should I sit here? I would have been exhausted a long time ago. And still I would have to sit here. I still don't know why I sit here, I'm still waiting for someone who can tell me why? Actually I have all these talks waiting for someone to tell me why. But I have no hope.

This is peace – the peace of mind that cannot decide what comes next which is already there. So, what to do?

Q [Another visitor]: As I understand, it is the subject that perceives all the objects?

K: No. The subject is already experienced by That what is experiencing the object. There's no need for it. It's just the way it happens.

Q: So, there are two sides of the coin, subject and object?

K: No. Subject-object are one side of the coin. The other side of the coin is the absence of the subject-object – presence-absence. In the presence there is a seer, seeing what can be seen. The other side is the absence of seer, seen, what can be seen. So, there are two sides of what-you-are. You are the Absolute Self – the coin, and one side of the coin is the presence of experience and the other side is the absence of experience. In the presence there is always a presence of the seer – 'me', experiencer, experiencing what can be experienced. That's the presence. It starts very subtle with the presence of awareness, but already there is an 'I'.

Q: The subject in this case is consciousness?

K: Consciousness is one side of you That plays the subject and the object. It plays all the roles. There's a conscious side and an unconscious side. On one side you are conscious in this dream of consciousness and the other side is the absence of the dream of consciousness. But you are in the presence and in the absence of the dream of consciousness. Both are your sides. So, you cannot get rid of the consciousness or the absence of consciousness.

But in consciousness, this is all there is – whatever you can experience. Whatever can be, is in consciousness. But what-you-are is with and without it.

Q: And the other side is the absence of consciousness?

K: The absence of whatever you can imagine.

Q: Who is perceiving it?

K: There is no 'who' in it. How can you experience the absence? How can you experience something when you are not there? That's why the absence is heaven. The absence is heaven and the presence is hell and that's the way you realize yourself. And now in hell you want to know what is heaven. Can I go there and be there? No. I have to tell you that you have to stay in hell. You will stay in hell forever. No one wants you in heaven. [Laughter] We don't need you in heaven – 'we'. [Laughter] So, what to do?

That's the joke that you think that you still can be there where no one is. You are seeking something what you will never experience. You knock on heavens door, but when there's no heaven, there's no 'you'. The knocker is gone – knocked out. It's like knocking on heavens door and no one can open as there's no one at home.

Q: 'My' experiencer that cannot be in absence...

K: Your experiencer? Show me that one. [Silence] You doubt it, so it cannot be true. All is fiction here. It's all a 'maybe', the moment you experience yourself it's a 'maybe' – all fiction. You will never know if it's true or not. You believe, it's hear-say, someone told you – that's all and you cannot take that. You need to be stable and sure, you need a reference point. Then you should not come close to me.

Q: I feel uncomfortable when I think – Maybe I was not being in the moment and I was involved in the good moments and the bad moments...

K: You need another master who can show you how to be more aware and more in the 'now'. Maybe you should go to Eckhart.

Q: No... [Laughter]

K: There you can resonate – they say.

Q: I saw his video and it was like a fish – without any emotions – cold...

K: Very fishy – that's called sell-fish. He wants to sell something and that stinks. He wants to sell you something so that's selfish – it stinks from the beginning. And by intuition you should smell it – by instinct – it stinks! The new earth stinks! [Laughter] This bloody power of now – stinks! The power of stinky now! [Laughter] I like to demolish all of that – fascist Eckhart!

Q: Fascist?

K: Come on! He wants to change the world! He says consciousness is not good enough. Consciousness has to transform into a higher level – that's fascistic. He is Franco and Hitler and Mussolini in one person. [Laughter] I like to make him a Nazi. I'm a German I must know what a Nazi is. I grew up under many of them.

So, my dear Nazis. [Laughter] Everyone who wakes up in the morning always has an intention to change something, wants to make things better today, has an idea of what is perfect, of how it should be and does not agree with existence – It should not be like this. You just have bullshit ideas. Any intention that has an idea of changing something – is a fascistic one.

The slightest idea that something is not right – is fascistic. But how can you not have that? It's never right. How can you accept that? There is no way of accepting experience of separation – from the beginning, no acceptance. And you try very hard to try to accept it. But it's impossible. So, the moment you wake up, you wake up in unconditional hate. Coming from unconditional love – from the absence, to the unconditional hate – the presence. Heaven and hell. These are the main ways you realize yourself. You realize yourself in heaven and you realize yourself in hell. The absence is the heaven side and the presence is the hell side. No way out!

Q: And it's okay?

K: It doesn't need to be okay. You just cannot change it.

Q: If I accept both?

K: It's shit. You cannot accept both.

Q: Why not?

K: Because then you would be someone who is apart from it. Then you would be different from it, and then you are born-apart – a Napoleon who did it. [Laughter] There would be two – you and heaven and you and hell. No! You are the nature of heaven and you are the nature of hell. How can you accept it? And who needs it?

Shit is everywhere, it was shit, it is shit and it will be everywhere – shit, shit. [Laughter] You know that. By nature you know it was shit, otherwise you would not sit here. It was shit, it is shit and it will be shit. I can just tell you that. What's the problem with it? If all is shit, it was shit and it was not good, it is not good and it will never be good enough – in this side of realization, it will never be good. So what?

You only suffer because you hope that one day it will be good. Because you have an idea that you will have a master that one day will make everything good and you will be enlightened and happy forever. And I sit here – you will never be happy! None of you! There was never anyone who was happy and there is now no one who is happy and there will never be anyone who is happy. Because the very idea that one exists – is unhappiness.

The nature of any existence – the famous Buddha said – All existence is discomfort, suffering. And I totally agree. Any experience is an experience of discomfort. And this is the way experience-side is – so what? And then there's another side of non-experience. The absence is heaven – every night in deep-deep sleep. And then you wake up in presence – shit! [Laughter]

Wherever I say that around the world, everyone lightens up.

If there is no hope of any future, if it's not going to get better, in this absolute 'Who cares?' [Laughing] – Shit! [Laughing] *Sat*-shit-*ananda* – every where! Having a troubled mind is shit, having a non-troubled mind is shit. Because both is shit. That's called mind – the idea of being divided.

Q: Can I accept it and leave it?

K: No. You cannot leave it. It will always be there. You have to be what-you-are, inspite of it. You are That! What-you-are has no interest in that. It cannot make you more or less satisfied as what-you-are. It's just never ending shit – as you are. The nature of shit is what-you-are.

And as you never started and will never end, the shit never started and will never end. So, this discomfort will be there forever. So what?

Q: Nothing to do...

K: Just have the next sip of coffee or whatever comes next. There will be no end to this. The next will be the next – that's all.

Q: This is what I meant by acceptance...

K: But for that you don't have to accept anything because the next will be there anyway whether you accept it or not. Forget acceptance and just be what-you-are. Because what-you-are never needs to accept anything to be what-it-is. The one that needs to accept, is a phantom and you may become a phantom that's closer to acceptance. But it's still – shit! Relative acceptance from a relative 'one' who accepts.

Q: So, Absolute acceptance?

K: Doesn't exist. No one can have it. So, what you cannot have, you should not be interested in. It's bad. Then they say you say all is shit and it's bad and then I see you and I don't see a person who is unhappy. I tell them, if you don't know happiness, that's just fine. You don't need to know anything and in that happiness, is just seen as another bullshit. If you don't have to be happy, it's not so bad. You don't have to be good, you always will be bad.

Q [Another visitor]: So, it's always going to be lonely...

K: It's always going to be lonely as there's no second. You will always be alone. [pointing to sleeping visitor] No hope, nothing that can be done, he went straight to sleep. [Laughter] He's exercising as a corpse, already.

Q [Another visitor]: Is absence same as deep-deep sleep?

K: Yeah. It's a pointer to deep-deep sleep.

Q: And you are the presence?

K: No. You realize yourself in the presence as you realize yourself in the absence. You are the presence in absence and absence in presence. There's no two. You are the nature of absence – which is the presence, and you are the nature of presence – which is the absence. You don't have to understand that. I just tell you that's what you are.

And that what is the absence has no influence in the presence, that's the problem. God cannot change anything in the presence because God is absence. In presence God is absent and in the absence he's the presence. But in the absence there's nothing to change. But where something could be changed, he's absent. So, he cannot change in presence or absence. Absolute helplessness!

The absence cannot influence the presence. Energy cannot decide how to realize itself. It can never be seen. So, energy is the absence which shows itself in phenomenal, whatever you can experience. The experiencer experiencing what can be experienced. But the nature of it is energy which is absent in all the three – the essence of it, which is the absence.

That there can be a presence, it can only be in the absence. That there can be a absence, it can only be in presence. And both are not different in nature.

Q: When you speak of deep-deep sleep, you speak of the absence?

K: It's just a pointer that everyone knows. Every night you are that absence. So, know yourself as you know yourself in absence and in the presence – what-it-is. Your nature does not change in anything. It's not that you should only stay in deep-deep sleep.

Know yourself as That knowledge which is with and without the knower. The presence would be the knower. But with and without the knower – you are. That's the knowledge of your nature. The nature That doesn't need to know itself. In the presence, there's a starting point of a knower and all relative knowledge comes with That. All the ideas of what can be known – that's called ignorance.

But you are also absence of ignorance, so you are the nature of ignorance. Just as you are the nature of knowledge – Absolute in both cases.

Q [Another visitor]: In the master-disciple relationship, I can see why that's duality. But isn't it possible that there's a shared awareness?

K: That's the question if the awareness can be shared. I'm more from tradition of Ramana, he never took any disciple. He destroyed relationships from the beginning including the master-disciple relationship. He said that's impossible. How can there be two? How can there be one who knows and other one who doesn't?

Just call it good company. In good company, there's no master and no disciple. In good company, there's only Self, there's 'I' to 'I'. So, there's no master and no slave and no one knows more than the other.

Q: When you say good company, you are making a concession to the language...

K: I just say what Ramana or Nisargadatta would say. I would not even call it good company. You can say bad company is where there are levels, there's one who knows more than the other – relative more or less. In good company, there's 'I' to 'I' – the Absolute to the Absolute – Self talks. So, it's not that you are less than me or I know more than you and I have reached a level of awareness and you have to reach there or I can show you the way. There is no way, nothing to gain.

Q: I was with a master and with him I had a realization which seemed to be connected with the master...

K: There are many realizations with masters, but they are all relative and they come and go.

Q: Experience comes and goes...

K: Yeah and realization is an experience. If you say it came because of a circumstance, for sure it will be gone.

Q: But doesn't that show you the truth?

K: That's the little hope that one day I will know the truth and it will reveal itself in front of me and the veil will drop and I shall be in clarity forever.

Q: There's a realization of the truth...

K: How can there be a realization of truth? The truth that can be realized has to be a relative one. It needs two – one who realizes something else. Even realizing himself is two selves. That's why it's called real-lie-zation. They are real lies and more or less lies. But every realization is a lie. They are not real, they are lies.

As deep as you can go with your realization, it's a lie. As profound as it can get, it's a lie – lie, lie, lie. Every master is a lie and every disciple is a lie. Whatever can be said is a lie, whatever can be experienced is a lie. Lie, lie, lie. The question is – was there any master who ever helped anybody? Do you really think the Self needs any help from a master?

Q: The realization is that there is a lie, that everything is formless...

K: But even that goes away too. Everything is formless, is that a truth?

Q: That there is no form...

K: Is that truth? Whatever you can pronounce and find out, would be covered again. Whatever you say now is separation because the non-form is different from form and formlessness. Then you make another level – emptiness. Then you say I realized that emptiness can never get more or less. Sounds good! Then the opposite of emptiness would not be true.

Q: But that's the nature of language...

K: No. You cannot escape in language. Don't blame language, you can do better. Many people come to me and claim that they have realized something. That they went to a deep place where no one was, there was just emptiness and there was no one to find. They really found a place where there was no one. So, is this not truth and that was truth? Who makes a difference – When I was not it was true and now when I am, it's true. Who makes this difference?

Q: I am not saying that what 'I Am' is not true. I am just saying that there is a realization that there is a constant or behind...

K: Behind what? You make two, just listen to what you say. Even That what is prior is different to that what is not prior. Whatever you say, you create two. Even absence and presence is two. The only thing that I can point to is, in absence and presence – who cares? You are in the absence as you are in the presence.

But you don't have to realize That. That's your nature. It never needed any other realization. It's realizing itself as the absence and the presence. Very simple. It is not any special realization that there is no form or anything.

Q: I had a master earlier and I had an experience in which I realized that I was losing him...

K: That's the nature of realization, that the master disappears because you are absolutely fed up with everything. It's like perception disconnects from everything. But I tell you, one is stupid enough to pick it up again and what gets less, gets more again. The strange realization of the Absolute Self you-are. It's sometimes less stupid, but it's still stupid. And the root thought 'I', you cannot get rid of. It's always present.

Susan Siegel was a good example of realization – losing her ego on a bus stand. Then she started to talk that all is unconditional love, we are all ocean of love and there is no suffering. And there's a little seed of fear but it's so small that it's not even worth mentioning. It will be gone sooner or later anyway. Then two years later, out of the little seed, it became an ocean of hate again, and then she died soon after that. So, this ocean of love is very temporary. There's still a seed of 'I' there and it will always grow again. It was cut down to the very beginning, as awareness. But that what can be cut down, can grow again and stronger than before.

So, the understanding that cuts it down, is a relative understanding that cuts down a relative problem – 'me'. Then 'me' really believes that there is 'no me'. Only the 'me' would say, there is no 'me'. The 'no me' will grow again. I just point out That what-you-are in nature, in Absolute existence, doesn't need you to realize anything. It was, it is and it will be what it was – with or without your realization.

Whatever you realize, however profound, however deep, your nature never demanded that. It's just a part of the story of one realizing something. Even becoming cosmic consciousness is still stupid. From the beginning till the end, whatever happens in this presence – is ignorance. Even the absence is ignorance. These are the two sides of knowledge – experiencing itself in the presence of ignorance and the absence of ignorance. The absence of ignorance seems more comfortable and the presence of ignorance is discomfortable. But what to do? You cannot not realize yourself.

And if one realizes himself as whatever, what about the consciousness in other cases? One is realized and the others are stupid as hell. How can that happen? A book came out – If You Wake Up Don't Take It Personal. But how can you not take it personally? You make it your story. Even a no-mind, a no-story becomes a story. You cannot help it, this phantom will have a story – once I was not realized and now I am a realized phantom.

Q: So, you don't have a story?

K: The phantom always has a story, but who cares if the phantom has a nice story or a bad story? It was always a phantom that was unrealized and whatever the phantom realizes, is a phantom realization. It's called fun-tom – have fun with it because it's a never ending story of a phantom who believes in himself and then believes in being realized or not realized. Who cares about an enlightened phantom? Only the other phantoms. It always needs a community of ignorant ideas and one of them maybe is a master-ignorant. The master of ignorance! There are no masters of knowledge. How can there be a master of knowledge? How can there be a master of Heart? You can only be a master of shit. [Laughter]

And I call it shit, because it is shit – compared to what is your *chit* – the knowledge, whatever you realize, whatever you know, whatever has a knower or can know – is shit. Even knowing himself, is shit – shit knowing shit. *Sat*-shit-*ananda*. Sometimes it's unavoidable, the phantom will always carry a story and sometimes it's a story of 'no-story' – the story of being unborn. Even that is a story. Even Osho's grave – never born, never died – is a story. What to do with it? I leave you my dream! Okay. [Laughter] Why not?

I like that there was never anyone who was realized. There are rare cases like Nisargadatta and Ramana who point to that. The Self is ever realized and what is not the Self – this image, this idea, whatever it realizes is stupid. Who cares about a realized idea or a realized image? Only other images.

So, there's nothing to do and one will always be stupid. It's only a question of more or less stupidity. The presence of more or less stupidity and the absence of more or less stupidity. But what-you-are is in neither of them – knowing or not knowing itself. It was always That what-it-is – That what is never-never. Call it an

Absolute dreamer, that dreams the dream of dreaming and a dream of not dreaming. The Reality will always realize itself, and cannot stop it – as whatever comes next. The most stupid and the most profound. What to do?

Rare cases say that you have to realize yourself. But everyone takes it personal. They tell you, you have to realize yourself. But they talk to what-they-are – Reality, and Reality has to realize itself – moment by moment. It was Reality realizing itself, it is Reality realizing itself and it will be Reality realizing itself, and there is no becoming in it.

Q: So, realization is connected with time?

K: You have to realize yourself in time. How else can you realize yourself? In an imaginary time. You are the realizer, realizing and that what can be realized – as that what-you-are. You experience yourself as all three – the seer, the seen, what can be seen – the whole presence. You experience yourself as the presence of the seer, the presence of the seen and the presence of what can be seen. The knower, the knowing, what can be known. The experiencer, experiencing, what can be experienced. But what-you-are can never experience itself as what-it-is.

So, it will always experience itself in separation. Even the purest awareness experience is separation. There is no other way of experiencing yourself. It's a dream of separation. That's the way you realize yourself. What can you do? And That what never started, will never stop. There is no hope that one day it will be over.

Q: It sounds like...

K: It sounds like many things. It sounds like Jesus when he says – 'Me and my father is one, but I am not the father'. It's like 'me' and 'awareness' is one – but I am not the awareness. Just pointing to That – you are That what-is. Like Nisargadatta says – 'I Am That', but not knowing what-it-is. But I Am That – That what is the knowing and That what is the not-knowing. The knower and the not-knower. You are That what is realizing itself.

And you will always 'be'. Wherever 'you' are, you will 'be' – That – which never comes, never goes. You are not that ghost phantom who believes that something has to happen. You cannot help experiencing yourself as that, because your nature is helplessness. You cannot want what you want, you cannot decide what you decide. You cannot realize the way you want to realize yourself because there is no 'one' who could want that.

In Reality there is no 'one' who has an idea, even the idea of how it has to be, how it should be. That already happens too late. So, even the now is too late. This bloody power of now, is bloody too late. The power of now – later. [Laughter]

Anyone else has any other deep, profound, something? I always feel bad when I have to destroy all of that. [Laughter] I am lying. What can I do? [Laughing] But I have to live with that guy too, he never allowed any bullshit in that way. The moment it came, it cut it off. So, I better be quiet. [Laughter]

Q [Another visitor]: I come here for entertainment...

K: That's the best what one can have – Have fun with the phantom. [Laughter] We are not serious-tom's, we're fun-tom's – fun-tastic, what the fun-tom comes up with. Again and again. Fantastic stories of big master-disciple relationships and sweet tra...la...la... and the fire from within, in the presence of *shakti* blah, blah, blah, the *shaktipats* and *darshans* unlimited. [Laughter] We can make a new company – *Dardhan* Ltd. [Laughter]

Q [Another visitor]: I don't know why I come for...

K: If at all, than it is for entertainment – nothing to gain, nothing to lose. If you remember something or not, it doesn't matter.

Q: Afterwards?

K: Even what you have done before. [Laughter]

Q [Another visitor]: Whatever you do, doesn't make a difference...

K: Maybe it makes a difference, but who cares? Maybe it does, maybe it doesn't.

Q [Another visitor]: But the story has a way...

K: It promises you happiness, but it never delivers.

Q: I don't feel like pursuing happiness or anything...

K: So, you are an expert of unhappiness. [Laughter]

Q: In the past I longed for enlightenment, but not anymore...

K: This locomotive is running out of steam. I tell everybody that there was never anyone who was happy. There is only unhappiness [Laughter] and they all laugh. Happiness can never be experienced. Thank God there is no happiness. What is the problem? Imagine there was happiness and you missed it, that would be something. [Laughter]

But you are not so unhappy that all there is – is unhappiness. So, it doesn't make you unhappy when all there is – is unhappiness. The only thing that makes you unhappy is that there could be happiness, and you missed it. Then you would never forgive yourself. Then there are these bloody masters who claim to be happy – kill them all – shoot them – at first sight – Pang![Laughter]. They are really sadistic.

When you have no idea of happiness, there is no unhappiness. If you have one idea, you create the other one. If you don't know what is there anyway, if you don't know what is sad, you are just sad. If you don't label it, you are just sad. Sadness is my true nature. [Laughter]

Q [Another visitor]: If you experience contentment...

K: That's unhappiness. From the nature which is happiness, whatever you can experience is unhappiness – even contentment.

Q: Happiness has a polarity with happiness...

K: Happiness that has a polarity with unhappiness, is as unhappy as everything.

Q: Is there any happiness without a polarity?

K: If there would be such a happiness, it would not know any happiness. So, it doesn't exist.

Q: It doesn't exist, but its there...

K: Where? If the Self would say something, it would say *sat* is fiction, not satisfaction. All there is is, sat is fiction.

Q [Another visitor]: Everyone is walking around pretending to be happy. Is that what is happening?

K: It's all pretending. They are pretending to be happy and pretending to be unhappy. If you just stop pretending and be-what-you-cannot-not-be – that's all. Then you are neither. Then there's neti-neti – neither happy nor unhappy, because you don't even know what you are and how you are. And you don't have to know how you are and what you are. That what needs to know what-it-is and gives it a name for sure is a definer and nothing is fine enough for that definer. He always wants to find himself and he is always pro-found. [Laughter]

Q: That's why you say – They are happy and I want to be like them...

K: They just want to make you jealous. They are bad! [Laughter] They are nasty people. [Laughter] Shoot them! Be generous and show the other people that you are not happy. [Laughter] That makes them feel good – maybe. If you show them how happy you are – it's like a war – Look you asshole, I can be happy!

Q [Another visitor]: So, it's about showing that you are unhappy?

K: It's the same. It's a competition between the two, who is more unhappy or happy. It's always a competition. Who is more beautiful or more ugly? Who is more realized than the other one? Competition on every level – everywhere. My master is better than yours. And if you have the same master, then you say my master loves me more than you.

Q [Joking]: I see him more...

K: I see under him. [Laughter] I am closer to his underwear, you just see his trousers. [Laughter] I am more aware as I see his underwear.

It's amazing, the competition never stop. The moment you wake up, even when there is no one around, you compete with yourself. There is already a competition, who is ruling today? The one who wants to wake up quickly or the one who wants to stay in bed? There are many definers waking up in the morning and everyone wants to be the main definer today, and has a concept of what is better for today – What to do. Competition! Who rules today? My mother or my father or me? My genes or my understanding? Out of what should I live today? Out of that – I am not? Or out of that – I am? What is my basis today? Then you start your baseball.

At first you have to remember what-you-are, a man or a woman. That's already a big decision every morning. [Laughter]

Q [Another visitor]: No, you just look under your blanket... [Laughter]

K: It doesn't work for everyone. [Laughter] What happens to a trans-gender?

Q: Then you are always undecided... [Laughter]

K: Okay. That was very spiritual. [Laughter]

Q [Another visitor]: You mentioned *sat-chit-ananda*. The *ananda* does not have a subject...

K: That's why everything is shit. When everything is shit, there is neither subject nor object. That is the *ananda* of shit.

Q: The *ananda* of *chit*?

K: The *ananda* of shit. If whatever is shit and you are it, then there is no one there that's not shit and That is *sat*-shit-*ananda*. Shit, shit,

shit. There is no opposite to it. If whatever is That what-you-are – That – call it Self. I like to call it shit. It's a good example because shit doesn't mind shit. You need to be someone who believes not to be shit – then it stinks. You need to be one who is non-existing absolute – the nature being separate, being apart – that stinks.

But if whatever is – is shit, Self is shit, God is shit – whatever you come up with is shit, then there is no difference in anything. Shit, shit, shit, shit, and that's *ananda*. When even *ananda* is shit, then shit is *ananda*. Then the next sip of coffee is as shit as next sip of – whatever. But there is no 'one' who believes that he is outside of the shit. Being inside of shit, is shit. Being outside of shit, is shit – shit, shit, shit. If nothing can give you any satisfaction… [Laughing] Because whatever you can get is shit.

Q: I am not talking about a 'you' wanting satisfaction…

K: Then what are you talking about?

Q: I am talking about *ananda* that is just is what-it-is…

K: Do you think *ananda* would call itself *ananda*?

Q: No…

K: You see. And whatever *ananda* experiences as compared to That what-you-are, is shit. It's a relative *ananda*, and 'relative *ananda*' for That what is *ananda* – is shit. Sooner or later, you will believe in shit. [Laughter]

To the Absolute knowledge, whatever you can know is relative knowledge. And compared to That what is knowledge, it's a knowledge of shit – doesn't mean anything. It's the same with satisfaction. Whatever can come and go, for sure cannot satisfy you. So, this shit cannot fulfill you – comes and goes. There is no satisfaction in anything, no fulfillment. None of these so-called relative experiences of fleeting shadows of coming and going can bring you anything. As it cannot bring you anything, it cannot take anything away. That's called peace.

It cannot make you more or less as what-you-are, and you don't even have to know what-it-is. You don't have to call it *ananda* or Self or anything. Even Self is fiction, *ananda* is fiction for what-you-are. All of that is fiction, or call it shit because you don't need it. None of them will unmake you or make you.

The quality of your nature is never more or less and can never become what-it-is – by anything. Now that shit happens, so what? It's a happening of shit. So, be it, as it is. And for That, nothing has to be realized – that's the best. You are by nature in the presence of shit and in the absence of shit – what-you-are. And That what-you-are never needs to know That – what-it-is. That what needs to know, is part of the presence and will never know what-it-is and will never know itself.

And whatever it knows is a relative knowledge known by a relative knower. The whole consciousness is relative and ignorance. What-you-are never needs it. You are with and without that consciousness – what-you-are. You may say that consciousness is your dream. But you are the Absolute dreamer which is with and without the dream what-it-is. Call it dream, call it shit, call it whatever – just be what-you-cannot-not-be – that's all. That never needs to be given a name or needs to be called itself as something.

And That will never know itself – that's the beauty of it. It never lost itself and it can never find itself. But the moment you imagine that you have found yourself as someone, as being born or anything – shit being a relative shit. Then your mother tells you that you are born and you are my kid, and their mother told them the same. And I sit here and tell you, it's all shit. Even they cannot help themselves, they have to tell you that. You cannot even blame someone. If you did not believe in that, no one could make you believe that.

It's all that you fall in love with the self – again and again – every morning, this bloody love. Fuck it all! But what to do? That's a fact that you cannot escape, and you fall in love again and again with all that bullshit. But why not? Does it make you more or less as what-you-are – no.

And now you start to hate it, otherwise you would not become a seeker wanting to get out of it. First there is loving, then there is hating, then there is loving again and hating again – never ending story of loving-hating what-you-are. The moment you experience yourself as a lover that is different from the beloved, you are in the misery of separation. From that, you are in passion of trying to unify yourself with the beloved. You uni-fight, uni-fight, uni-fight. You worry about yourself, love-care about your beloved self.

You cannot even help it. Even by trying not to care, you care about yourself. If I say shit happens, I mean it. You don't need it for your nature, but still you have to experience yourself as that. There was no one ever who escaped that. So, no one ever made it, by anything. Not Jesus, not Ramana, not Buddha, not Mohammad, not Zarthustra, not Osho – no show.

That's the best, no one ever made it. There was never anyone who was realized, or unrealized – that's the beauty of it. If there was anyone who was realized, it would confirm the one who is not realized – that's the hell. When Buddha said there was never any Buddha walking this earth, that's the meaning of it. If you meet Buddha around the way, kill him. Buddha will never show up – your nature will never show itself as anything. It's a dream of nothing.

The only thing that I can confirm to you is that, you will never make it. And I never met anyone who made it, and I never met anyone who didn't make it.

Q [Another visitor]: You realize in waves but it doesn't last and you want it to last...

K: It happens to many, nothing will last – or everything.

Q: But still the feeling is pleasant than being involved with the mind...

K: Yeah. Mind sometimes minds and sometimes doesn't mind. Mind not minding is more relaxed and minding mind is not so relaxed. But it's still mind. So, sometimes there's mind, sometimes there's no mind – never mind. It's always changing, after good times come bad times, after bad times may be no good times. Where there ever good times? How can there be good times? How can there be good time in separation? It's a contradiction in itself – good time. It's impossible.

Time means separation, time means two, time means birth and death and all what comes with it. How can there be a good time? And if there is no good time, not even no-time can be good. There is no good, good is fiction. Like *sat*-is-fiction – everything fiction. So, *neti-neti* – nothing is neither good nor bad – all is fiction.

Q: The more mind is deprived of identification, the best it is...

K: It just takes another reference point. First it is involved in the personal one then it takes a reference point of an impersonal one. It shifts to another reference point. It feels more detached and being detached feels more comfortable. But it depends on being detached – sounds good. It is like in Zen Buddhism, you sit by the wall and have a *satori*. And suddenly your perception disconnects from the body and there is pure 'I Amness', where you don't know your beginning and your end – like space. Then it's no-time, no-form, no-nothing.

But the moment you want to stay there, you are back in here – in the first (state of consciousness). It's more pleasant there than here. So, it's natural that you want to stay there. But the moment you want to stay there, you are out. There is no wish allowed in that – no control in space. The moment you want to control, you are out of it.

Q: So, there is no way to stabilize in That?

K: No. It's just another way of experiencing yourself, it's just different. It's less discomfort. Then awareness is lesser discomfort. It's like going into the awareness *samadhi* where there is not even no-time. Then you are in the third state – time, no-time and then you are the screen where time and no-time, form and formless appear. Then you are awareness – even better – superior consciousness. The most pure – like a screen where all the projections, space and all of that appear but you are always okie-dokie. So, KO (Knock-out, first state), OK (second state), and okie-dokie (third state).

But just as you land there, you have to depart sooner or later. You have to go from no-time to the state of timelessness, to the *samadhi* of pure awareness. But the moment you come back here, you are as thirsty as before. It's just another way of experiencing yourself. Then you even go prior to that – being inspite of presence and absence of awareness. But then you wake up again. You cannot stop realizing yourself.

Q: Endless process?

K: Endless jumping from one reference point to the other – shift, shift, shift. You are like a sailor that is shipping all the dimensions of the universe and cannot land anywhere. All the dimensions are only there because 'you-are'. And you are discovering nothing new because it was already there. And wherever you land, you depart again.

If you cannot be in this hell of separation what-you-are, you will not become it in any dimension. This is the worse – I agree. Nothing is worse than being a relative human being in a relative time having a story. If you cannot be in this circumstance what-you-are, what is it worth to be what-you-are?

If what-you-are needs a special circumstance, its depending on a special circumstance. So, still you are a relative, depending, phantom. But what-you-are never minds to be in whatever, whether it's here or there because it doesn't know any difference. For what-you-are, there is no difference in nature. And what knows a difference, is for sure not – That. The phantom is always hunting the impossible. It will never catch himself – but he may try. It's always a Mick Jagger – I can't get no, but I try. Then there is another one who claims – I got it. Ha, ha, ha [Laughing]

It's really a joke if someone tells – I realized my true nature. If they even listen to what they are saying, they should start laughing about what they just said. What kind of bloody nature would it be that can get realized by you?

Q [Another visitor]: There is a school of non-duality that says – Do you know who you are? But you say that you could never know who you are, so it's a useless question...

K: Even that question is wrong.

Q: Or the question – Do you know your true nature?

K: It's all wrong.

Q: So, you can never know it?

K: Never. The question from Ramana actually was – Am I? And not – Who Am I? And the nature of the question is the nature of the answer Am I – I Am. It's like a stream of – That what-you-are. Even if you don't pronounce 'Am I?', there is a natural answer 'I Am' – Am I – I-Am. It's not – Who Am I? And then being the background or That what is prior. That is very personal.

Q: Some say do you know your true nature?

K: Know yourself as That what is the nature of the question and the nature of the answer because the 'Am I' is the 'I Am'. You are the 'Am I' and the 'I Am' – You are That – Am I–I Am is very natural. You don't even have to pronounce it. But the question 'Who am I?' for me is too personal and it always creates one who believes that he is beyond.

Q: So your natural state would be 'to be'?

K: That would be your natural state – to be 'Am I – I Am' – that's your nature that 'you are'. But you will never know what that is.

Q: You can never realize That?

K: You will never realize That. You are already realized, you cannot realize yourself as more than you really are – you-are – and there is nothing more to realize. That is why – Am I – I Am. It's not like – Who Am I – and then being the space that is the answer of the question. No! You are not the answer of the question, you are the question and the answer. Because nothing is different from you – You are That.

So, you are the question and the answer. But you are not the – Who Am I? And then the fake silence that remains. That's why everyone is so pleased with that question – Who Am I? The world drops, the spirit drops, the awareness drops and still I Am silence that is always present. Then you land in that silence which is different. Then they say, stay in that choiceless awareness of silence, know your true nature, abide in it – blah, blah, blah – bite in it. [Laughter]

That what needs an effort, for sure cannot be your nature. You were, you are and you will be – Am I-I Am – just that. That's what Ramana says – the basic sound you are – That what-you-cannot-not-be. That what is in the absence – the presence and in the presence – the absence. That there can even be an absence, you have to be. That there can be a presence, you have to be.

But that what is – That – you will never know. It is not an object that can be known, and you cannot know because there are no two.

Q: But can it be experienced?

K: Absolutely! There is no presence without the an experience of what-you-are, and no absence without That. There is simply no memory in absence, that's all. So, your whole story is only in the presence. But the absence is as much – what-you-are, as the presence. And there is an infinite eye, the infinite Self that is realizing itself in presence and absence. You are That, but you are not something that can be realized or be known by someone in anyway as a new knowledge.

It always was, is and will be – That – what-you-are. There is never any new realization, or something drops. That's why Wei Wu Wei talks about the open secret – without 'you', there is not even a secret.

Q [Another visitor]: When I ask myself this question, it does not transform into 'I Am'...

K: How do you ask?

Q: Am I...

K: And what is your answer?

Q: I don't know...

K: Then you don't do it right. You have to ask the question – Am I–I Am. Didn't you listen in Moscow? Was the translator so bad? It's a meditation. It's not a question in which you find an answer. The question is the answer.

Q [Another visitor]: How do you know that what Ramana said was better translated as – Am I?

K: There was this so-called realized guy from Ramana called Sadhu Om. He was Tamil and he knew more what Ramana said in Tamil than the English translators. He always said that the translators made it – Who Am I? But in Tamil he said – Am I? That makes much more sense to me. And I sit with people in Bombay who say that 'I Am That' is all wrong. All the esoteric stuff in the book that you have to be earnest and things like that Nisargadatta never said. And that is the biggest esoteric book for the seekers.

For years I said that if he really would have said that, then even Nisargadatta said bullshit. Who needs to be earnest and who needs to be honest? Then in the last book you find contradiction – Yes you may, but by all what you do or don't do, you will never know what you are. So, yes you can but by whatever you do, you can never attain what-you-are. You can be earnest like hell, but existence doesn't care.

And if it's meant by totality that the dropper drops, it will drop anyway. It's already dropped. If the devotion of the devotion happens so that the Self is the Self without knowing or not knowing, just by being what-it-is, then it will happen anyway inspite of whatever you understood. And all your understandings or all your realizations or all your profound insights – are worth nothing for That.

If that has to happen, it will happen. It's always inspite all what happened before – never because. What-you-are is never because of anything else. So, yes, in the dream you can reach some deep understanding. But all of that – bye, bye – sooner or later will be gone. And that's the essence of Yoga Vashishta's whole teaching – yes, you can understand and learn and realize but – see you next time! Whatever you gain now, you have to lose again.

There will always be a consciousness presenting itself as sitting somewhere and there will always be someone trying to realize himself. There will always be entertainment – infinite inquiry, but it will never be found.

June 9, 2012. Morning Talk.
Mallorca, Spain

You pretend to be someone and I'm too lazy to pretend – that's all

Q: Can I say that I am not the phantom?

K: I have no idea what I Am. If I say I am not a phantom, I would still be a phantom. I better have no idea of what I Am. The only thing you can say is that you are not an idea, but whatever you say, it will be an idea – a concept. So, what you cannot talk about, one should be quiet. But can you be quiet? No. So, we can talk about it.

Q: What can we talk about?

K: We can talk about what you are not.

Q: What is the difference between what you are in relation to us?

K: There is no difference.

Q: Is there some kind of understanding?

K: No. There is no difference in nature and in the dream, the relative experience, there are so many differences we cannot count, but in nature, there's absolutely none. In the phantom world of ghosts, every ghost is like a snow flake – always original, an expression of what is life, always different.

Q: They always speak about the presence...

K: And the presence is always different every moment. That's why the present moment is always different. And what is different is changing and fleeting – you cannot fix it. It's dream-like fleeting shadows, coming and going. But what-you-are, never moves.

Q: Can we as the phantom end the duality?

K: No. The phantom cannot become what is the Self.

Q: So, why am I trying to become a happy phantom?

K: If you try to be a happy phantom, you are the unhappy one. I have nothing against you trying to be a happy phantom, but if you ask me, I don't care.

Q: But I care...

K: Yeah. But don't make me care. [Laughter]

Q: Yesterday you said, I should not fall in love again...

K: I did not say you 'should not' fall in love again. I said you cannot avoid falling in love again. You have to be what-you-are inspite of falling in love, because falling in love, you cannot avoid. Every morning you fall in love with the experience of whatever is there – love at first sight. Then loving caring happens – naturally. There's nothing wrong with it. Just be inspite of it and see that loving caring will never lead to the fulfillment.

There is a tendency for happiness, but the happiness will never be there. You will always love and care about yourself but it will never deliver the happiness you're looking for – never ever. Happiness can never be experienced or owned by anyone or achieved. So, happiness cannot be attained by anything. It will always be bad – bad, bad, bad! It was bad, it is bad and it will be bad. What to do?

That's peace. The rest is hell, of the worrier. The worrier expecting that by his doing he can get happy. I can talk about the relative one. and I can say that with the understanding that everything is bad, you may achieve the peace you are longing for, but if you expect the peace to happen in future, you make it a relative object in time which is fleeting.

Q: Yesterday I was asking whether I can get happiness...

K: It's bullshit. It has to be bullshit. You are always trying to be happy and when you are happy you fear that you will lose it again. There is no happiness in time – never was.

Q: But I do feel that there will be happiness in future...

K: But you have lost it already. So, why bother? If you want to suffer, go for it. I have no problem. You ask me how to stop suffering and you want to continue. I have no goal of stopping you, I have no interest. If you want to continue suffering because you want to survive as a phantom, do it.

Q: How can I avoid being a phantom?

K: By just being what-you-are.

Q: How can I be what I Am?

K: How can you not be what-you-are?

Q: I know that I Am what I Am...

K: So, be That. You ask me what you can do and I tell you be what-you-cannot-not-be. I cannot tell you more. Whatever you try now, you want to make it as your advantage and then you are in hell again.

Q: I know that I am not the doer...

K: Of course you are the doer. Now you are the non-doer, even worse! I know you listen to the non-doership teaching. This non-doership is not for 'you'. Now you understood that you are not the doer and now you became a non-doer. Now you define yourself as one who has not done anything. You just take the opposite – just for survival and that's the same bullshit.

Non-doership means there is nothing ever done. Nothing was ever created, nothing ever happened – that's non-doership. Nothing was ever done by anyone or not-done. It's not that I am not the doer. You just shift from one reference point to the other – just for survival and I sit in Bombay with all the left overs of Ramesh and I have to tell them. [Laughter] Everyone that's left over is a non-doer now. [Laughter] – I am the non-doer, nice cozy place. It's all done by God. Fuck him, but don't fuck me – doesn't work.

But it works, that's the problem. You understand and you try to make the understanding work for you. That's the problem. And whatever works is wrong – from the beginning. If it works and makes you a little bit more happy, it's wrong. because it confirms that there is 'one' who needs to be more happy. Succeeding is really putting oil in the fire of hell.

Q: But I never succeeded in anything...

K: You said that you understood that I am not a doer. That's already a success. Now you're sucking from that understanding. Who says that I understood that I am not the doer? It seems like you landed somewhere, where you understood something and now you make it your understanding. So, that's succeeding in an understanding and now you try to make the understanding work for you.

This bloody success, sucks forever. It's an incest – with yourself. Fucking yourself from this side to that side. Before you were fucking yourself from this side to that side and now you fuck yourself from that side to this side.

Q: So what can I do? What can I 'not' do?

K: Nothing. You just said you are not the doer and now you ask me what can I do? You see how schizophrenic it gets? [Mocking in Italian] Schizophrenia *infinate* – tra...la...*latte* [Laughter]

It's a joke. You just have to listen to yourself and then you just see the joke of what one is thinking.

Q: I never laugh, I am a very serious person. That's my problem...

K: You have to work on that [Laughter] You need to join the silly sisters anonymous group.

Q: For a while I thought that I am a phantom, so who cares?

K: Don't ask me, I don't care. Imagine if I would care, I would run around like a messiah and tell everyone – that you are not a phantom. I go to a butcher and say, you're not a butcher. You never butchered a pig.

I'm not a Messiah, I don't want to change the world. but if someone asks me, I have the fun of destruction – until the nitty-gritty. This is substrating whatever can be substrated and what is left, is what-you-are – the absolute leftover – the absolute abstract who cannot get rid of itself. From there, you're reality, realizing itself in the next bullshit – if you like it or not.

But first you have to go to the nitty-gritty of the absolute leftover, you are and by being the absolute leftover, the abstract itself, the substratum, the noumenon, That what-you-cannot-not-be, from there on you're That what is realizing itself. It was, it is and it will always be – That. And for That, nothing is too heavy and nothing is too light. There is not even a question that you're delighted by yourself, that you need happiness or sadness. It's just – you are That! Never began and never will stop realizing itself.

So, you are the *Parabrahman*, the absolute leftover, the substratum, then you start dreaming. The first is dreaming yourself as a dream object of a dreamer and then dreaming and then all what comes out of it.

Q: I read a book and it said that there is a bright light there and there is nobody there. Is the bright light also consciousness?

K: Of course, everything. Whatever circumstance you enter, you just enter a different stand point or a reference point. You go to many different dimensions and you die in all of that because it's called – die-mansions. It's not the home you're looking for. It's all die-mansion. You die again in an idea, a circumstance. It's all a cemetery. The whole dimensions of all kinds of light and bullshit and space and all that you can imagine – it's all cemetery. It's all dead experiences – dead, dead, dead.

The doership is the cemetery of life and the non-doership is also the cemetery of life. Whatever can be said are dead words anyway. The only solution is that there's no solution for anything. What-you-are never needs any solution because it never had any problem. That what-you-are doesn't even know itself, how can it have problems? And that what knows itself, will always have problems – infinite problems.

The biggest problem is that there is no problem. That's the biggest problem for that what needs problems. You create problems which would not be there without you – just for survival. That's what you were just doing. It's quite obvious, but that's what everyone is doing here. You are not alone.

Q [Another visitor]: Can we talk about the idea that the phantom has about something to be solved, something to be reached, something more…

K: And that will never stop. It will go on forever because consciousness is a phantom and consciousness will go on forever, looking for itself. You only think about this little one here. This is consciousness in one tool trying to know itself, but consciousness has infinite tools of trying to know itself. The inquiry of consciousness doesn't stop here [pointing to the body]. It's everywhere.

So, the inquiry will never stop and if in one case, if the tool rests in some understanding, what about the consciousness in all the other tools? So, don't take it personal if peace happens in this bullshit body-mind, what about the rest of them? And who cares if one bloody body-mind understands something? What kind of understanding is that anyway? A fleeting, relative, bullshit understanding – any understanding.

But everyone is selfish here. What can he do? He loves the next [moment] more than himself. That's what the Bible says – Don't love the next more than yourself. That's the root of suffering – love.

So, my dear lovers [Laughter]

Q [Another visitor]: My beloved ones...

K: I would not say that. [Laughter] At the most I can say is – dear lovers. [pointing to a visitor] What is your idea of *bhakti*?

Q: Melting of the lover with the beloved...

K: He has no idea but he repeats some Osho things.

Q: I don't know what it means...

K: So, why did you tell me that you see *bhakti* here?

Q: Who sees the *bhakti*?

K: You told me that you see *bhakti* and you don't even know what that means. So, now I caught you.

Q: That what knows what *bhakti* is, you would immediately kill because that would be relative...

K: But seeing *bhakti* would be relative too. So, why did you tell me that you saw *bhakti*?

Q: Just recently...

K: I see you're fishing in the dark. It's amazing there are so many concepts about *bhakti* and *jñani*.

Q [Another visitor]: So, what is *bhakti* for you?

K: In the Indian tradition it means the unselfish action for your *guru*, without expectation – but no one can do it. Never ever there was anyone having *bhakti*.

Q [Another visitor]: That you can say about *jñani* as well... [Laughter]

K: No disciple can have *jñani* the *guru*.

Q: But who needs a *guru*?

K: You.

Q [Another visitor]: You're the anti-*guru*...

K: I'm not even an anti-guru. It's like doer and non-doer. But it's a good example that everyone has here-say information from books and they're talking about it.

Q [Another visitor]: In case of Radha-Krishna, *bhakti* means dissolution of separation which is compassion. Krishna cannot-not be compassion.

Q [Another visitor]: But he [Karl] would deny...

Q [Another visitor]: He cannot stop being compassionate. He doesn't even know he's compassionate...

K: Whatever you say I deny it anyway. [Laughter]

Q [Another visitor]: *Bhakti* means dissolution of sense of separation...

K: No. [Laughter]

Q: That's what it means with the *gopis*...

K: It's all go and pee [Laughter] It's all a fairytale of *bhakti*. The nature of *bhakti* is no different from the nature of the *jñani* – that you are inspite of the presence of the sense of the separation and not separated by the sense of separation. But it's not the dissolution of separation. You repeat what comes out of relative teachers with a relative understanding of *bhakti* and then they think that this sense of separation has to go for you to-be.

No! Only for a phantom something needs to go. You are inspite of the presence or the experience of separation – That what is never separated. You are *bhakti* not knowing *bhakti*, and that what can be described as *bhakti* – for sure is bullshit. What can be described as a *jñani*, is the same bullshit. The moment there's a *jñani* knowing a *jñani*, there are two *jñani*s too many and when he tells me there's *bhakti* in my eyes, I tell him shut up!

I should be the frustrated one. After so many years, whoever repeats what I say is wrong again, because you want to put something together, because you want to make a statement, it must be wrong – from the beginning. You want to make it right? [Laughter]

Q [Another visitor]: But you're pointing again and again to the same pointer, that's compassion...

K: I don't need to know what compassion is, I just have fun.

Q: He doesn't know...

K: I don't need to know it. The moment I know compassion, I kill it.

Q [Another visitor]: What do you mean, when you say the moment you know compassion, you kill it?

K: The compassion you can know is bullshit. You kill it, out of fun – just by being what-you-are. It's not because you need to kill it, it's fun to kill that bullshit. It's like a duck, the idea of compassion comes up and you shoot it. Not because you need to shoot it, your nature is shooting it.

Q [Another visitor]: Who is shooting it?

K: I don't know. Just by being what-you-are, you shoot everything – because you are the Absolute hunter, hunting whatever can be hunted – shooting it and then hunting the next one. An infinite never started, never ending job of hunting yourself. It will never end, it's just the fun of hunting. It's like a sport.

Ramana said the same when people asked him – 'Why are you talking when you know that there's nothing to do, everyone is already what one-is and nothing happens'. He replied – just for sport and I totally agree with it. Nisargadatta gave the best explanation of why one talks. It's like you have a full bladder and you have pressure in your bladder for a while and by accident you go to the toilet and pee. Then you feel that peeing is not so bad, you enjoy the peeing. From that moment on, you just pee. You pee where you are – because it's the joy of peeing. That's the joy of talking, the joy of whatever. It doesn't need a special reason, you just enjoy what you do. When you're a hunter, you enjoy hunting. That's the joy of irrelevance that you hunt without being hungry, without any necessity.

That is the meditation of what-you-are. The nature of meditation is – there's action without intention. There's no cause in it, it's not be-cause. It's just – Pang!

Q[Another visitor]: How do we get to where you are?

K: That's the problem, you cannot get there. You're already there.

Q: But how did you…?

K: I don't know. Did I do something special? [Laughter] I can tell you millions of times, what happens there is no different than what happens here. I drink coffee as you drink coffee and the next will always be the next. What's the difference?

You pretend to be someone and I'm too lazy to pretend – that's all. It's laziness! Your nature is Absolute laziness.

Q: But how did you get there?

K: You cannot become lazy. You're already lazy and now you're so exhausted because you pretend that you have to do something. That's what makes you so exhausted. This little effort. I fuck it all and by fucking I don't get exhausted because I don't want to get an orgasm out of that fucking. I don't want to have a result out of it, nothing has to come out of it. There is no baby coming out of that fucking – no result. It's just fucking.

Q: But before that?

K: There's no before, it was always like that. How can there be any before? You were always the absolute fucker, fucking from all directions – and there's no baby coming from it – no consequence – that's the beauty of it. Whatever you have done, is being done now or will be done, has no consequence for existence. There is no consequence. Nothing ever happened – but still you have a dream of fucking and you will be fucked.

In India there was a message written on the back of a rickshaw – 'No one remains a virgin, sooner or later everyone gets fucked by existence'. No, you cannot become That what-you-are, you were always that and in the presence you are That consciousness which is the fucker, the fucking and the fucked – you know that. It's the total fuck-tory of presence – consciousness being the penetrator, vibrating in the infinite vibration of the whole universe. Energy reacting to itself in so-called *karmic* consciousness, never ending *karmic* consciousness.

The only *karma* that's here is the *karma* of consciousness – as a reaction to itself, moment by moment. An absolute reaction to itself. So, did anything happen in that? Did consciousness become more or less? Did any baby came out of it? Or any realized consciousness? Was there any unrealized consciousness? Or consciousness is just pretending to be unrealized and the next step would be to pretend being realized?

Consciousness is the big pretender, playing all the roles. Actually it gets all the Oscars, the best role, the best director, the best stage. The name of consciousness should be Oscar.

Q: That's from Karl's experience...

K: I am That and you are That. So what?

Q: Who cares?

K: You care. What-you-are never cared and then – you pretend to care. So, you care but you don't care that you care. It was always like that. There's maybe a story of a caretaker, so what? It's a beginning of a story and an end of a story – a fairy tale of a shadow caretaker which came and will be gone. So, it's not even here now.

It's like a chain of pearls put together as a chain of reactions. Now you hang it around your neck and you think it's 'my' story – I did it my way – I'm Frank Sinatra. It's all playing. You play with it and now the play becomes serious. What's the problem? Now you play being unrealized, now you play being not enlightened, now you play that this is my body, that you have something.

Did something happen by that? You play an owner but you're

not the owner. You play the owner. You play the owner, you play the owning and you play what can be owned. You play the lover, you play the loving and you play the beloved. It's a play – and it will never stop.

Q: Play well...

K: You cannot play well – it's all bullshit. You play to be shit, but you're not the shit. Every moment you believe you're the body, you play to be shit, because this [pointing to the body] is shit. It was shit, it is shit and it will be shit – believing in this food body. It was food, it is food and it will be food.

Q [Another visitor]: But yet there's no intention?

K: There's intention, but there's no one who has it.

Q: When you say consciousness is...

K: Stupid! Absolute stupid. It's stupid because it's in love with itself in an imaginary love affair and that's stupid.

Q: Something is creating that intention...

K: It's not creating, it was always there, an intention of love that you wake up with. It's not created, it's already there. That's the way you realize yourself. It's never created.

Q: It's amazing. Look at the body for instance, the intelligence, the beauty, the design is incredible...

K: Shit! That's the lover talking about his beloved.

Q: But it's there...

K: And when the next wrinkle comes, it starts to cry, [Laughter] and if the make-up is gone and the boyfriend runs away and the beautiful kids don't do what you like, this bloody beautiful body disappoints you from the beginning. It's a disappointment. You thought you have an appointment? But you have a disappointment. [Laughter]

The nature of this body is disappointment. It was so promising that it may give you some pleasure in life, an orgasmic feeling and ecstasy, but what happened? All disappointment – from the beginning till the end – shit happens. It's a shit machine – a beautiful shit machine – my body. Right now you're a shit machine, you know that – especially after breakfast. [Laughter]

Q: It's amazing, the body carries two pounds of shit...

K: And the rest you don't count? [Laughter]

Q: We can't see that...

K: I see it totally – fifty five kilos of shit.

Q: How much is that in pounds? [Laughter]

Q [Another visitor]: How many stones?

K: How stoned are you that you believe in this body? How drunk from an idea are you that you believe in this body or in beauty? How stoned can you be that you left yourself? And for what?

Only love can make you so stoned, so pretending. You played with this puppet house of Shiva and now you fell in love with the puppet and now you yourself became a puppet. Now you try not to be a puppet but as more you try not to be a puppet, you confirm that there's a puppet. This trap is absolute!

You just played with it and now the play became serious – shit. Now the shit became more real than That what-you-are. What a bullshit happened! How can that happen? Only love can make you such an idiot. What else can make you such a big fool that you take this shit more real than what-you-are? And you think that you depend on that shit – your relative life. It's unbelievable, but that's the wonder of stupidity.

As absolute knowledge you are in nature, as absolute stupid you are in your realization. As much absolute knowledge, as much absolute ignorance. In realization, you realize yourself as absolute ignorance. And there's no other way and part of it is believing in this bullshit body. That's part of the ignorance and you cannot help it. You have to be inspite of that because you cannot stop it. This intention, this loving caring about yourself, this stupidity, being stoned, in this ecstatic drunkenness of yourself which makes you believe in all that bullshit, you cannot stop. You're helplessness and you cannot resist yourself.

So, you cannot realize yourself in that ignorance. What to do? And to call it beautiful is just a pill, an attempt to make it a bit relaxed. You try to make it more bearable for yourself. But what is the reason? Who needs to bear something and call it something and call it not so bad? That you can even tolerate this. It works for a while but it's just a temporary medicine. And all the medicine just confirms that one is sick and you're love-sick from the beginning – sick of love.

That's why you listen to the sad songs so much because they all talk about the love that went sour. In that sense sadness is quite profound – always an open door.

Q: Is there an open door?

K: Depression seems to be eye of the needle. You want to push yourself through it but you cannot enter it with anything. You have to be as-you-are and by being that you're already beyond the eye of the needle, but you cannot take something there.

But you want to take your body, your mind, your spirit. You want to take something home, but you cannot take anything home. You have to be as you-are – nakedness itself and that is your nature – the absolute absence of whatever you can imagine. Just by being that, you're in the kingdom, but there cannot be any king. You would just be joking to believe that you can rule your kingdom.

But now you want to rule your kingdom and you want to call it something – beautiful or something – your kingdom… ha…ha… ha… You are king-doomed, by trying to become a king. By being a body, trying to understand consciousness, trying to understand existence – you want to rule it, you want to be the ruler and you will be punished by that – by being the most lonely bastard in the universe – just by trying to rule yourself.

But what can you do? Out of loving caring about yourself, you want to control your beloved; and if you cannot, you even get jealous that it may do what you don't want. Then you get angry. There's total anger inside that your beloved is not doing what you want. The anger of God – that the beloved is not behaving. Angry bastards! [Laughing] I like to talk to myself like that. [Laughter] Actually it's not 'my' self, but anyway. I lie to the bullshit self – just-in-case. It's fun to talk to what-you-are and tell yourself that you're the absolute bastard – you know that – *bastardo absoluto*

Q [Another visitor]: And prior to consciousness?

K: You can say with and without consciousness. Prior, I don't buy. Nothing is prior to anything. You are with and without the experience of consciousness. That doesn't mean you are prior to it. You are with and without realization – That what is reality. You are with and without realizing yourself – That what is reality.

You are not prior to anything. If you say you're prior to consciousness, you make it separate again – special. That's why I don't like 'Who Am I?' where 'you' become the prior. You are That – Am I – I Am – whatever that is and for That, there is no before and no after and there's no second. You can never escape That – what-you-are.

Being prior, is just another escape, or being the witness, being the screen, being whatever you talk about is just to make it a little more bearable and I sit here to put more weight on your shoulders so that you totally break into infinite pieces – piss off.

No. I'm not here to make it more bearable in anyway. I'm not here for anything, anyway.

Q [Another visitor]: This concept about God is fun. Everyone talks about it, there are television programs about it and there are debates about it, but no one is actually thinking what is it?

K: If you ask the Pope, he can tell you. [Laughter] He's sitting on the holy chair. God speaks through him. [Laughter] Now God has a German mask. [Laughter] It cannot get worse, I tell you. That's why it's called Vat-i-can – What I can do, I will do. The holy Pope, popping everyone – very popular. [Laughter]

Everyone talks about God. Some believe in God, some don't believe in God. The ones who don't believe in God believe more in God than the ones who believe in God. The non-believers are sure that there is no God. And I say – just-in-case.

Q: They believe in something formless...

K: They believe in the Holy Father. No. It's like a pill. If you believe in it, you can sleep better.

Q: We're not supposed to question them on those things...

K: No. You're supposed to question it but you have to talk with the right people, who can give you the answer. Don't talk to any Tom, Dick and Harry. Talk to the experts. It like a guru tells you, don't talk to the co-disciples what I tell you, talk with me. Be quiet about what I said, if you have questions don't talk to your stupid colleagues.

Q: There are so many teachers, so many *gurus*. But we never hear it clearly as we hear it from you...

K: Because I have nothing to gain here. Normally teachers have something to gain. They want to keep you as a disciple – as a slave. It's like a SM(Slave-Master) connection. Guru-disciple connection is like master and slave connection and you cannot even say who's the master and who's the slave, because normally the slave creates the master.

The disciple calls someone a master and makes him a master. So, you don't even know who's creating this slavery. It's a co-dependency, that's a master-disciple relationship. One can only be there because of the other. Then they celebrate the relationship because as long as there is a disciple and master, you can survive in that ignorance.

Q: First I have to declare him as the master only then he's my master...

K: You are on top of the master. You decide who's your master and then you discuss with others, who's your master? My master is much better. [Laughter] You always compare your master.

Q [Another visitor]: Is it because of wish of the people that there is something more?

K: No, it's fear. Out of fear, you want to have some help from a bigger guy. It's all fear. The moment you exist, you're in an existential fear. Then you create a God by that – a higher authority, grace, all those ideas come from fear. And fear comes from the false evidence that you exist, with the belief that you-are.

So, the moment you exist, you create the imaginary hell. Even all the wars happen because you believe and you fear and you fight for truth. People tell you this is the right way and then other people say the opposite and then you fight them. Even in little groups there's fight about truth, because you think you need truth to exist. It's all fear and then you try to fight for peace and that will never stop. So, keep fighting.

Mahabharata is a nice story. You have to kill people, you have to do whatever is asked from you because it has already happened. What can you do or not do? Always pointing towards the helplessness of your nature. There is no one who can change the way realization happens, and if it's meant for you to be a murderer, you will be a murderer. If it's meant for you to be – whatever – you will experience yourself as That.

If it's meant for this guy to sit here and talk the things that normally you cannot talk about, you have to do it, if you like it or not, but it's not better than anything else. In that sense – may it be as it is. This is the best wish you can have, because it's an instant fulfillment. Why wish for anything else, if you can wish that what fulfills you instantly? If you wish for something – may it be as it is.

Q: Why do you say 'May it be'?

K: Because it's a wish, how can you say it otherwise? Otherwise you would say as if you understood something – it is like it is. You have to wish for something. You cannot not wish. Even not to wish is a wish. If you have to wish at all and you always have to wish, make the wish – May it be as it is, because you cannot not wish and it's already fulfilled. You don't have to wait for fulfillment – instant fulfillment. It's bullshit but – sounds good.

Q: It sounds like a *mantra*...

K: It is a *mantra*. And it stops your mind in a way, in the moment. It's like the wish wishes for wishlessness and the wish is already there, where it belongs.

Q [Another visitor]: Can a murderer wish not to be?

K: He can wish, but he still has to murder.

Q: We are here because?

K: You are here because you don't want to be here. You don't want to exist, that's why you exist and because of that, you're here. So, you don't want to be here, that's why you're here.

That's like God. She was just lying back and the light went on and she woke up – somebody here? [Laughter] That's called co-working. [Laughter] You just relax and the light goes on and you are back. You ask where does that come from?

Q: You just used the word 'relax'...

K: God was relaxing and then a switch behind him goes on and then he's astonished – where does the light come from? And already he's back in this business here, because then he's wishing to know – 'Where the light came from?' And then by trying to know where the light came from, he becomes the one who's here.

Q: It's like a play. The puppeteer controls the puppets and the characters think that something happened. But from God's point view, he's just doing his job...

K: And that you would like to be that? [Laughter]

Q: No. You used the word relaxing...

K: I didn't say relax. I said when God is relaxing, someone starts the switch and the light goes on and already he's in the next trap because he wants to know where does the light comes from?

Q: Maybe it's a particular kind of neurosis...

K: God knowing himself is already neurotic.

Q: If you have a particular pattern that you don't like about yourself and you want to change it...

K: That's everybody.

Q: For me, I changed my pattern. Now there's more relaxation...

K: Maybe now there's less energy as your body gets older. [Laughter]

Q: I reckon...

K: There's nothing to reckon, that's just the case. [Laughter] If I talk to eighteen year old seekers they're more enthusiastic and energetic. Now I talk to all the leftovers here, they have much less energy [Laughter]

Q: When you say the murderer has to murder, I find it difficult to accept...

K: You don't have to accept it. You want to employ it and right now you cannot find the tool of understanding that can give you an advantage. So you cannot accept it. If you could employ it to your new pattern, you would just employ it and accept it. Now it doesn't fit into the pattern of what you are, so you don't employ it, you cannot work with it. So you don't accept it.

But even that you cannot decide, what's your pattern and if it fits or not, but it doesn't fit now, so you don't understand it and you don't take it. It's not in your hand.

Q [Another visitor]: The way you sound – shit, shit, shit, I'm wondering why go on? Why not kill each other?

K: Try to kill the shit. As I said, you tried to kill yourself infinite times earlier. You killed yourself right now by believing that you exist. That's the only suicide you can attempt. You're already dead, kill yourself, I have nothing against it. How can you die more?

Q: You can…

K: You've killed yourself already and you'll kill yourself again – again and again. The suicide is every moment you are not what-you-are – you're dead. Any moment you're not That light which doesn't know any light. Any moment you believe you're born, you're dead. How can you kill yourself further? You've already did that to yourself. In that sense, what's new?

Q: It sounds like agony to some people…

K: Let them be in agony, dead people should be in agony. I have nothing to change. Why should I try to make this cemetery a better place? For who? It was, it is and it will always be a cemetery. Every experience, every circumstance is a cemetery. So what to do?

I can call it shit or I can call it dead, call it empty, call it whatever. Shit just comes naturally in this case [pointing to himself]. It fits in India because *chit* means knowledge and this [pointing to his body] is shit. It's a joy of shit. It's a joy that it cannot give you anything. It cannot make you more or less as you are, it cannot give anything, it cannot take anything away. Shit, shit, shit…dead…dead…dead…

It's a dance of the dead, so what? It's fun. If you dance good or bad, it's dead anyway.

Q [Another visitor]: Yesterday you talked about what Lao Tzu says that the Tao that can be told is not the true Tao…

K: I would agree with him.

Q: Yet in Tao Te Ching he talks about the lesser Tao that applies to worldly affairs like governance…

K: It's a wrong translation. [Laughter] I know it because I had to listen to different opinions for the book, my publisher had a different opinion. In India, they have a different opinion and in every translation there's a different attitude. One is more for the world and the other one is for the beyond and you cannot decide. Maybe they're all wrong. If you look for the right translation, you will always find something that fits to your pattern of understanding. Then you think – that is better than the other one.

For me all that is wrong. Finally, even the whole book is bullshit. For me, this is Tao Te Ching because we can talk about what-you-are-not – it continues. It's all Tao Te Ching – talking about what-you-are-not. Because whatever we say, what-you-are, what existence-is, is-not. You cannot employ Tao Te Ching for the worldly business – for sure not.

Q: It's being done, from martial arts to governance of countries, to medicine...

K: They all employ it for their purpose. But you cannot blame the Tao Te Ching that the intention of it was that someone can employ to take it to employ for his purpose. It's like the church employing Jesus. But you would really think Jesus would be a Christian?

Q: But Lao Tzu himself talks about governance in Tao Te Ching...

K: Let the government do what the government is doing. Just be what-you-are inspite of what the government is doing. But it's not that you can change the world or you have to change the world.

Q: But he talks about the wise governor being non-actoral...

K: But he's not talking about the government. He's talking about God being the absolute governor – not caring about how he's governing or what happens with his realization or his world. That's being the right governor. Being what-you-cannot-not-be, the absolute governor, not caring about the results of his non-action.

It's like meditation, you act without expectation. That's the right way of meditating or doing an action. Like Buddha said –

action without an actor, means actions without expectations of what comes out of it. Not doing action for results – just acting out of – no one knows, for what?

It's not like a little personal gain for some future goals and results and payments. So, he talks about all of that – the right way is that there is no way to reach what-you-are. Buddhism is not different, even Advaita in essence is the same – Just different angles of how to look at it.

I was doing karate for twenty years – with the empty hand and now I do the tongue karate – with the empty tongue. First I started with the material, the empty hand and now it's the empty tongue, empty words, empty questions, empty answers. I liked karate because the one who dies wins. Dying means you are not there, you are the absence and the absence always knows a split-second before the other person attacks. And the reaction is always faster than the action out of a mind, the action of attacking. Fantastic! Sometimes two persons would stand for half an hour and nothing would happen, then they would say, both won. The one who attacks, loses – instantly.

I Am what I Am – the absence and whatever you try to do, to attack me [Laughing] – try harder. I like everything [Laughter] only because I don't need it. I like everything only because I don't need to like it. There's no demand That I have to like it, but I like the dislike as much as I like the like – don't get it wrong. But I hate you all! [Laughter] Unconditionally. Whatever you do, I hate you anyway. Then you can do whatever you like.

That's the beauty of hate. You can do whatever, you can hate them anyway. For love, you always have to work and find a reason to love somebody. But hate is natural. You even hate that you exist. And then there's someone else that you hate equally. That's the nature of presence – hate. It's fun.

And if everything is hate, it's unconditional hate. So, in nature it's absolute, but if there's hate and love, that's hell.

Q [Another visitor]: But there are certain rules that are described in the book like the Vedas which help you to get the results...

K: Vedas is different, Vedas is technique, vedanta is technique.

Q: Are you saying these techniques are not worth spending time upon?

K: I didn't say that. If you want to run the washing machine, maybe you want to read the manual otherwise you wash your delicate clothes in high temperature and they become very small. [Laughter] In that sense, if you want to have less wrinkles, you use the right cream. It depends on your goal. If you want to have a relative goal, just read the manual. And the vedas are manuals, like the ten commandments.

They are manuals for daily life – don't kill your father before he fucks your mother. [Laughter] That's practical. But if you don't want to be the baby of your mother, try to kill your father before he fucked your mother – but that's impossible. But for esoteric people, everything is possible. They do regression and go before the father made love to the mother. That's why they go before, to redirect the future.

Q: To choose the father...

K: Yeah, they choose it. I chose my – underwear – this morning – maybe. [Laughter] Because that one was the only one which was clean that's why it was my choice.

Q: So, are all these manuals for the Self?

K: No. There are no manuals for the Self. There are only manuals for shit. So what do you want to say?

Q: It's gone...

K: That's why I make all these jokes and then the question is gone without being answered. [Laughter] So, it's gone anyway – inspite of your action or me answering it, it will be gone anyway.

Q: Maybe it would come back...

K: Even if I would've answered, it may have come back. There's no guarantee in anything. But sometimes the question gets answered, sometimes not and they will be gone anyway – answered or not, doesn't matter. Most of the times when you get an answer, you create ten other questions out of it, it's just feeding the questioner.

Q [Another visitor]: They say most of the problems in the world are because men cannot have babies and they are jealous of women having them...

K: Good for them. Do I have to comment on it? [Laughter] I think the western man is happy that woman takes this job. Actually the ladies take every job now, they drink more, they smoke more, they beat-up people more, they're more aggressive – but they still have to have babies. I heard they don't need men anymore because now they can make it out of their own eggs, they don't need sperm anymore. The babies come out of themselves – without men. That sounds good – We are jobless! [Laughter] No one needs us – unemployed – fuck yourself. We don't pay anymore.

Q: They say men have forgotten to be men, but for women it's easier to know who they are because they give birth...

K: Good luck babies! [Laughter] Actually I'm not so jealous. Even if women know who they're, that's bullshit. It's more bullshit because then there's a woman, who knows who she is. Shit! Should I be jealous that they know more shit than me?

It's like they have a near death experience while giving birth. The pain is so immense that sometimes they're out of the body and have near death experience. It happened quite often when there was no anesthesia. In that sense, the ladies should not have any anesthesia, they should have pain of the lifetime so that they may disconnect from the body because of that pain.

And then you claim that they know who-they-are because they have had this out of body experience? It's like a *satori* that you get by sitting in front of a wall for ten or twenty years. And then the pain in your legs is so immense and your Zen master hits you so very hard, that your perception disconnects from the whole circumstance and you're in that oneness space. Sounds good!

But whoever went out, came back. How many concepts do we have? How many advantages of being a woman or man? It all makes you feel bad.

Q [Another visitor]: You said yesterday that *Parabrahman* creates the universe...

K: It's dreaming this universe, it's not creating it.

Q: But it dreamt the universe in one instant?

K: In one instant – the dreamer, the dreaming and what can be dreamt are there – in a blink of an eye. When the Absolute eye wakes up, everything is there in a blink of an eye. Out of the Absolute potential wakes up, in a blink of an eye, all is there – whatever can be. Out of the Absolute potential as a *Parabrahman*, as the Absolute potential of all existence, in that waking up, the whole potential wakes up – as final.

All possibilities, all events are there – instantly, because they were already there in the potential of *Parabrahman*. As they're already there, it's unchangeable.

Q: If every possibility is there, in a pre-determined way, isn't there a choice between possibilities?

K: No. That's the nature of *Parabrahman* because there's no second, he cannot control himself because for control or making a decision, it needs two. Then the decider has to be different from that what he's deciding. But in absolute absence of a decider, the definer, there's no one who can decide anything. There's not even a possibility of deciding anything.

But when he wakes up, everything already is final – finished. So, there's no decision, nothing to do anymore, everything is already done. And it's too late to change it because it's impossible to change that what's finished.

Q: So, our perception of time is just an extension of the blink?

K: You just have to experience yourself in all relative ways and all absolute ways. The relative way is that you have a dream of coming and going. That this moment comes and goes, but in coming it doesn't come, because it's already there and in going, it doesn't go. It's just like a frame of movie which is infinite. The frame does not go by going and not come by coming. You just experience one aspect of yourself – moment by moment, but the aspects are never born and never die. They're not created, so they cannot be destroyed.

All of That is what-you-are. Every single aspect, every single moment is infinite in its nature – infinite life – eternal life. Experiencing eternal life moment by moment as every moment in its nature is eternal life – never created, never can be destroyed. The dream is that in coming something comes and in going something goes. In birth nothing is born and in dying nothing dies. That's all!

So, as this moment is never born, it cannot die. It's like – frame by frame, you have to experience yourself – dream fragment by dream fragment. But it doesn't mean fragments are coming or going.

Q: So, is it just that the illusory 'I' that is moving across the panorama?

K: You are the unmovable spectator – the Absolute 'I' – the Absolute seer, who's experiencing itself frame by frame coming from illusionary future and going into an illusionary past. But you're not moving. The frames are coming and going in front of your eyes. Then you make a movie out of it, with an imaginary movement.

You're not moving in it. Never! It's an imaginary movement of frames – moments coming and going. But even to know all of that, you better know yourself what-you-are in nature – That never needs to know the mechanics. It's magic in a way! Just enjoy your show – by being That what is trying or not trying anything – just to realize yourself.

This is one aspect of realizing yourself in a personal camera position. When you're the space, there's already no reference point. And then you experience yourself as awareness, there's not even space or time. Even that is a fragment of what-you-are and then the experience of beyond is another movie – an absence of a movie – it's part of the movie. And the impersonal awareness which comes, then the impersonal being a human. All the seven different levels of the movie are permanently there. You just shift between all those possibilities which are already there and never come and never go. There are seven different variations of dreaming yourself or experiencing yourself.

And none of them is better than the other.

Q: Does that relate to what the esoteric people call the seven?

K: Yeah. The people from Theosophic society have a seven. In every so-called system, there seems to be a seven. It's logical – there are three personal ones – 'me', the personal spirit and the personal awareness – my body, my spirit, my awareness. And then going beyond, the ownership disappears. Then you're the Absolute awareness, the Absolute spirit and the Absolute man – just by being That.

But all the seven are seven different ways of experiencing yourself and none of them is more or less better than the other. So, the seven makes sense. This is also the experience of mystics of all times. You have to transcend all of them, because none of them is your true nature.

Your true nature can never be found in one of them. They are just seven different ways of experiencing what-you-are. But there's no way of knowing yourself in one of them. So, you're neither personal or impersonal or beyond.

So, this neti-neti, implies everywhere – neither that or that or that – all of the seven cannot deliver what-you-are. You haven't lost yourself in one of them. As you've not lost yourself in one of them, you cannot find yourself. But you try.

You have an infinite house, you have infinite rooms. You go to the rooftop, you go to the penthouse, you go to the cellar, or the health kitchen. Maybe this is a health kitchen, everyone wants to go to the fridge and wants to be the first – living in a commune – that's really a health kitchen.

All that what we called world and family and relatives and having relationships – all of that is in the room of health kitchen. You meet the devil and the grandma of the devil. All these stories and then comes the next one – more stories.

Q: When you say this way is not different...

K: It's in quality not different from the other. The only quality in all the ways is – you-are-That! What can get not more or less in whatever way. You're the quality experiencing yourself in differences. But by none of the differences, you can gain or lose anything and none of them can deliver what you're looking for.

They all promise. At first the world promises satisfaction, then the spirit promises satisfaction, then the awareness promises, then the beyond promises, then the impersonal promises. They're all promising, but they promise something that they cannot deliver – to know yourself!

And your seed of longing is always to know yourself. But none of them can deliver. You fail in all of them – to know yourself. That's what Buddha talks about too – being the absolute failure. He went through all the possibilities and none of them delivered what-he-was. So, the Buddha nature cannot be found in any of that way – so there's no way, the way is the goal.

And you cannot not look for yourself because by loving caring about yourself instantly, in the presence, you look for yourself –

wherever – the inquiry will never stop. You will always experience yourself in restlessness – no rest. You cannot find the rest you-are – in anything. The rest that you find, you have to lose again. So, it's a relative rest – in all of those seven – is relative rest, but it's not the rest you're looking for.

So, the peace that you find in any one of them, will be a relative peace – the peace that's different from something else. The peace that you can find, you land in, you have to leave again. So, in the absolute way – peace off – and be what-you-are inspite of what-is or what-is-not – may it be as it is!

However it is, it cannot make you more or less as you are and it cannot deliver what you're looking for. But you still have to look. The looking cannot stop. This paradox, you cannot understand. Many had this absolute insight – that they cannot find themselves, but they ponder why is this inquiry still going on? Why am I still looking? Why don't I stop?

How can you stop? You have to realize yourself – whether you like it or not – inspite of being what-you-are. And because you are, what you are – reality – you have to realize yourself. The nature of the *Parabrahman* is the Absolute dreamer and he cannot stop dreaming, beacuse the moment he tries to stop dreaming, he's part of the dream. And That what is part of the dream, is impotent. If the almighty had the wish, he could stop the dream.

But as the almighty cannot have a wish as there's not even one who can have a wish. But the moment he's in a dream, he's absolutey impotent – absolutely has no power. The almighty in the experience of having no power. And now you're angry that you have no power, because you already know that you're the almighty, but you cannot do anything – it's a schizophrenic position. Shit!

So, when I say shit, I mean it. Shit! I'm the almighty, but I cannot use it. I cannot control anything, even by being the almighty. Even inspite of being the absolute dreamer, I cannot change the dream which is already finished. So, what to do? That's why all the sages sat somewhere and said this most common sentence – what to do?

And then whoever comes with an idea of what to do – they would say – try again, try harder.

Q [Another visitor]: Why such a waste of power?

K: It's not a waste of power because nothing happens – energy cannot be wasted. When the *Parabrahman* wakes up, nothing wakes up because it was already there. So, there's nothing to create, so there's nothing to waste. That's why it's inexhaustible – the whole universe, the whole thing is so inexhaustible, because nothing happened. And nothing changes because it's a solid block of what-is. So, there's nothing to waste.

This is eternal life. [Whistling with a bird singing in the background]

Q [Another visitor]: So, what do you think about the future?

K: There's a future which is already there and the past is not gone.

Q: So, it has already happened?

K: Nothing happens. All the experiences of the future, you will experience them again and again. This moment is infinite and you've already experienced it inifinite times. And last time, you had the same question actually and I gave you the same answer. It's a *deja vu* – again and again. Nothing comes, nothing goes. You will end up here, again and again. You don't even move from this moment.

Nothing moves, nothing comes, nothing goes. No coming in coming, no going in going. You're stuck eternally to what-you-are. [Laughing] You are the absolute addict to That what-you-are. And you cannot stop being addicted to That what-is, because you are That!

But you have to experience yourself as a junkie for That. But it's junk. The idea of Self is junk, you know That. Whatever you can gain, is junk and if you expect something that comes from junk, you become a junkie. A junkie means you're looking for the key of heaven, but even heaven is a junk, compared to what-you-are.

June 11, 2012. Morning Talk.
Mallorca, Spain

You cannot be burnt down by your own fire – but you try

Q: I needed to know when there is resistance...

K: Yeah. That's French! [Laughter] When you think of resistance, immediately comes France. [Laughter]

Q: So, what is resisting?

K: Who is resisting what? What is resistance? Maybe you can call it – the resistance as a little function of the 'me'. Always tries to resist, tries to control. Always wants to have it his way. Always resisting existence. This little resistance – this little blockade, trying to block everything, trying to have it his way. This little French inside. [Laughter]

Q: Is it also part of...

K: Yeah. It's part of the ignorance, of the dream – resistance. Because when there is two, you resist the other one. You want to control it. So, resistance is part of control or fear. It all comes together. If you come down to the basis, it's always fear. It all comes from the existential fear and you'd rather control your surroundings before your surroundings control you. That tendency is permanently there.

So, from the false notion of separation, you try to control. Because you fear that something can happen to you, by someone else or by something else. Then you try to resist, you build a defense system. Then you resist everything.

Q: So, it's not an energy, it's just an idea?

K: No, it's a function. A function of a phantom to resist – to be controlled. If you come to the basis of all tendencies, it's all existential fear. So, what to do? In the beginning God knowing itself, it has a potential of fear. Because there's one who knows himself, so there is something that can be doubted. There is a doubtful existence and from that doubtful existence, there comes all doubtful resistance, that something can be doubted. There's a doubtful existence and from there comes doubtful resistance.

All that whatever you can call – evolution or revolution. All the things come from that, trying to control something. And the control comes from the false idea that you exist as a relative object in time and then comes the whole story. So, it's natural for the phantom to resist.

And when I tell you, you have to be what-you-are, inspite of that phantom resisting or not, I just point to the fact That what-you-are is absolutely independent of the phantom resisting or not. So, resisting will always happen. Resistance cannot be destroyed because this is part of the relative world – everywhere. So, what to do? Enjoy the resistance and enjoy the non-resistance.

It's stupid, but what to do? Trying to get rid of the stupidity, is even more stupid. You always make it worse – in a way and don't believe in anyone who says, 'I don't resist anymore'. [Mocking] Ha, ha, ha. Then you can say, he resisted, resistance. And then he is more born-apart or Napoleon [Bonaparte], because he's special. Because he made it! He doesn't resist anymore! He accepts whatever-is! [Mocking] Ha, ha, ha – sounds good.

That's why I always say – sounds good, but it's not sound enough. It's depending on – whatever. It's another kind of conditioning. Just another concept of how it has to be and how it could be. Did you ever go to Douglas Harding?

Q: Yeah...

K: The headless way. It's like he lost his head by being a pilot somewhere.

Q [Another visitor]: So what do they mean when they talk about total acceptance?

K: When you talk about total acceptance, that's your nature, That does not need to accept anything. Only relative acceptance needs action – and showing it and proving it. The absolute acceptance doesn't need to prove that it's acceptance. So, it doesn't come into action. It's just acceptance. It doesn't even have to accept what-is and what-is-not. It doesn't even know anything else.

The nature of the Self is acceptance because the Self doesn't know the Self or anything else. Perhaps knowing what it is and what it is not – then there is acceptance. But in acceptance, there is no two because there is no need of accepting someone else or something else. And the relative acceptance always tries very hard, but it never succeeds.

So, the closest you can come to acceptance is – that you accept that you can never accept – as a phantom 'me'. No way! You can always have a high acceptance limit or tolerance limit. But there will always be a bigger camel that will come and step over your feet and your whole acceptance and tolerance will be gone in one second – Pang!

Q [Another visitor]: What I Am is both presence and the absence?

K: You're the absence of the presence and the presence of the absence.

Q: You told me yesterday and the day before...

K: You don't have to remember, you are That anyway. Don't try to remember, just be That. Don't make it a concept, I just point to something. When I say – you're the absence of the presence, I just point to the fact that you cannot be found in any presence. You cannot find what-you-are, because you are the absence of the presence. And in the absence, you have not lost yourself because your presence cannot be lost in the absence.

But now in the presence, you're the presence which cannot be found in the presence. By whatever present moment, you cannot find yourself. If you can find yourself, you could be something that could be found and that already is hell. Now you found yourself. You claim that you're a human, you know yourself and that already is hell.

So, you better be the absence of any idea of what-you-are. Because what you can find are ideas, concepts, sensational images and all kinds of experiences. But in all those experiences, you cannot be found. You cannot find yourself in the experiencer, experiencing, what can be experienced. If you really look for yourself, you cannot find yourself anywhere. No way to find yourself. You pretend that you're in the experiencer, but if you really look for it, you cannot find yourself.

That's actually Nisargadatta's Ultimate Medicine – look for the speaker and you cannot find that. By not having found who-you-are, you just remain in the absence of – what? You're not even a loser. Because if you would have been a loser, you could have found yourself. As you could not lose yourself, you're neither the loser or the finder. You're just – who knows? Who needs to know? But still you are! The laziest you can be, which has never done anything. Never active or inactive, neither doing or not doing – neither.

That's the famous neti-neti, you're neither that or That and That never needs to have any idea about acceptance or tolerance. Acceptance, tolerance only apply to the phantom concept world. Love, hate, all needs someone who calls something – something and has an idea about something. And that's the root thought 'I' – that always creates problems which would not be there without it. That's called mind.

Q [Another visitor]: I wanted to ask you something and I came across a poem of Kabir that seems to express the questions better than what I have. If I could just read it...

K: Yeah. I like Kabir. Anyone has something against it? [Laughter] Because I cannot drink beer, so I like Kabir. [Ka-beer][Laughter]

Q: [Reciting the poem]

> *There is a strange tree,*
> *which stands without roots,*
> *bears fruits without blossoming.*
> *It has no branches and no leaves.*
> *It is Lotus all over.*
>
> *Two birds sing there:*
> *One is the Guru and the other the disciple.*
> *The disciple chooses the manifold fruits of life*
> *and tastes them*
> *And the Guru beholds him in joy.*
>
> *What Kabir says is*
> *It's hard to understand*
> *The bird is beyond seeking*
> *And yet it is most clearly visible.*
>
> *The formless is in the midst of all forms.*
> *I sing the glory of the forms*
> *Because I cannot sing the glory of the formless.*

K: That's what I said, without the absence there would be no presence. It's different words.

Q: About singing the glory of forms...

K: That's what I say, I'm singing the glory of forms. You can enjoy them because you're not part of it. You like everything because you don't need it. That is the singing of songs of glory of informations that give you pure joy, because you don't need it. Because they cannot bring you joy. That's the joy of emptiness of forms.

Your nature, which you can say is the joy that doesn't need joy, is enjoying all informations of... And no one needs them. It's a dance of information which is pure joy because there is no need for it. It's a pure entertainment of life, but it doesn't need to make sense or anything. You don't get more or less by any of this information. So, they're pure beauty.

Q: So, there is in a sense a natural information of That coming from there [closing his fist] to rejoicing beauty...

K: It never stops. It's not rejoicing because the absence never dies and the presence is permanently dying and is re-born. So, this moment dies so that the next moment can be born. Because this moment died into the absence, into the hidden and something else comes into the front. So, there is death and birth – permanently, but what-you-are is not gone by something going and doesn't come by something coming. It's a permanent death and birth experience. It's a total construction and destruction. It's like Vishnu and Shiva in persona. There is no difference.

Q: When you were saying that *sat-chit-ananda*, it's all shit...

K: Yeah, but that's the beauty of it. Shit or emptiness or that it cannot bring you anything, for me it's the same. If one would not be shit, then you really make something shit. All is shit, all is equally shit – empty, cannot bring anything. Then it's fine. Then there's not even shit because you who sees everything is shit, is part of the shit. You're That what you see.

So, everything without exception, there is nothing what is not shit – including the seer. The seer, the seeing, what can be seen is *chit* or shit – doesn't matter. The shit is only there when the seer is different and not shit, seeing shit. There is no exclusion and then shit doesn't know shit and there is *sat-chit-ananda*. That's the happiness of shit – not knowing happiness and not needing it.

Q: It's like a dance without a dancer...

K: Yeah, there is a dancing, knowing, but there is no ownership in it. That's the main thing. Without ownership, who cares if it's shit or not? But if you own shit, then you're in trouble. If you're shit and you experience shit, then it's life experiencing life. Call it life, call it whatever. I like shit. If you use beautiful words, then you call it life and beauty and all that, the dance of life, the dance of energy and all that. Okay. Then you swim in it.

But if you can see it as dance of shit because nothing is left later, it all will be gone. It is easy to let shit go. It's easier to let shit go than beauty. I just want to make it easy. I can call it beauty, but just for the sake of making it easy. It will be gone one day – whatever you call beauty. It will be gone.

But if this is shit and shit follows and if it was shit, it is shit and it will be shit – Hello-good bye – it's just a piece of shit. But if you call it beauty, your attention is too fixed on that. Then you think you miss something when you're not giving attention, because maybe you miss one part of the beauty. But you would not miss shit. Just to make it easy. I can give it another name, I would not care. For me it doesn't matter and I don't say that out of compassion, I call it shit. Just to make it easy.

I like Kabir more than Rumi. Rumi is very romantic, it's not my type. Kabir is more direct, Rumi is behind the bush somewhere, in the heart of God.

Wherever 'you' are, there's shit – you know that. It's here shit and wherever you're not, it's the same shit. Where the awareness people are, there's double shit. [Laughter]

Q [Another visitor]: But we like it...

K: Because they're like Freud. They like to analyze shit in unlimited ways. It's like Austrian people. Nine years ago, I was in Vienna, I thought I would never go back here. Two hundred people in front of me, trying to kill me. [Laughter] Attacking me verbally. You still have glasses, you cannot be enlightened. You wear a watch, you cannot be enlightened because you still want to know what's the time. Bullshit questions and I thought what's going on here? They were attacking me from all sides and my master is a master of light and you cannot be like him.

And after two hours, I said it was like it was, but if you don't see me anymore, don't miss me. Bye bye. Then two hundred people started clapping – Bravo! That killed me. [Laughter] They were just checking me out with all those possibilities and saw that I survived. [Laughter] And since then, I have to go there. Now they're okay. [Laughter] But they were all attacking with all possibilities, from the lowest to the highest. Like a machine gun.

Q [Another visitor]: I have someone below me who's schizophrenic, trying to kill me...

K: In London?

Q: Yeah...

K: London is the most dangerous place. [Laughter] Was it a woman?

Q: Yeah...

K: I heard the same, all the girls in London now beating up everyone. They get drunk and they beat up everyone. I'd never go to London, that's too dangerous. [Laughter]

Q: I had to evict her, because my tolerance ran out...

K: Because the energy ran out. When you're full of power, it's easy to be tolerant, but when you're a bit older, it's not so easy.

[A visitor drops a bottle]

Q [Another visitor]: Sorry....

K: There's no sorry for that. [Laughter]

Q: It wasn't me, it was the bottle...

K: It wasn't me, it was the water. [Laughter] What a bullshit excuse. It was not me, it was the knife. [Laughter]

Q [Another visitor]: You were speaking of absolute block of what-is. Does it come with all possibilities?

K: It comes with everything.

Q: And all the possibilities of each person?

K: Each person is just a part of it, a fragment of the total block. It comes with whatever you can imagine. Whatever can be and cannot be. Instantly by that absolute waking up – Bang! – It's there. You can even say this moment is absolute in absolute action and it's a potential of all possible futures and pasts. So, everything is here and now – infinite now.

Q: For no reason at all?

K: It's just a realization of reality. That's a reason enough for me, at least. It doesn't need any reason to-be. It's just a pointer of peace, that nothing ever happened. That everything is already there and nothing comes and nothing goes. Nothing is born, nothing will die. Just pointing to the eternal life which is this, what you just experience.

Q: Why not call it silence instead?

K: That is silence. Silence means nothing comes, nothing goes. There's an imaginary movement – that's all. There's an imaginary noise. It's all imaginary, from a reference point of a you, you can call something whatever – noise or movement. But from That absolute reference point of what-you-are, which is life itself, nothing ever happens. There is no coming and no going and no birth and no death, in that what is called life. That's called silence and this is what-is – here-now, That what you just are.

And right now there is an experiencer, experiencing, what is experienced. The seer, the seeing, what can be seeing. The whole scenery is the totality itself. The only dream is that you as a seer, believe or imagine that you are different then what you see. That's the ignorance you're in. That's the only ignorance.

It's like, you're a puzzler and there is a big puzzle in front of you. You think you're the puzzler, who is different from the puzzle. But actually the puzzler is part of the puzzle. But the puzzler is always missing one little piece of the puzzle – himself. It's crazy! And sometimes during the day, you forget that you're the puzzler and naturally you become one with the picture. There is no difference between you and the picture, because then there is no puzzler and no puzzle.

And then there is a disturbance and then you're out of it. Then you're puzzled again. Then you want to find out why is the puzzler, puzzled. Something is missing. So, by imagination you become apart from the puzzle and then you're puzzled. Then you become a seeker. Then you want to find a way out because it's unbearable to be different from the puzzle. Then you want to go back to the oneness and be one with the puzzle. But as much as you want to be one with the puzzle, you're different. Crazy!

Q: It's more like forgetting then remembering...

K: Many times of the day, you just forget that you-are. Then there is not even existence, you just don't even know what happened. Then suddenly, you remember that you-are. Then you're out of it again. Then you become a member, by your memory. Then you make your story again. You spin your story from yesterday and tomorrow and today.

But in most of the presence, there is not even time. No coming, no going. It's just an automatic – you don't even know what it is. Maybe five percent of the day, there is disturbance, that you're out of it, there are problems. And then, you're the puzzler. If you're more than five or ten percent, then you end up in a mad house – already, because your nervous system cannot take it. Then you're already paranoid and schizophrenic, all that what you cannot take. You end up needing some downer.

Q: Then how can all these memories associated with the puzzle, come back to me when I wake up?

K: Because they all belong to the body. All the cells of this body are a cluster of energetic functions that have a memory. It's not yours. You just wake up in a memory, but it's not your memory. It's the memory of the body. The memory of your brain cells. If you have a demense, a chemical reaction in the brain, where is the memory? But still you-are what-you-are. There is no memory anymore but still the body is there and you are there. It's like the hard disk is erased, just by chemical reactions. So, where is the memory? Just a functioning in your brain.

The last words of Nisargadatta were, now with the body, all the memory, all the stories, all the tendencies and all what belongs to this body, are leaving me now. But there is still no one who cares. So why do you care about it? Because you fell in love with that story. It's like in a cinema, you want to know how it continues...

Q: You want to make it work...

K: You're curious what will happen next. The curiosity keeps you [making heavy breathing sound of a dog]. Then God becomes a dog because the dog wants to know what goes on – watchdog. What is the ending of the movie? And how does it continue? And can you stop it? No!

So, God becomes a dog. Just being curious what the bitch is doing in front of it. What to do? So, you become a lover and loving caring happens about – what about the story? You wake up every morning in a love story. Very passionate sometimes, sometimes boring, always different. Actually every morning you wake up in someone else. It's not exactly the guy you fell asleep with. Every morning is different and during every day, there's a different personality. A different mask appears – different aspects. You're never the same. You try very hard to do same as yesterday so that your friends should recognize you. You always have to remember that I'm like that, I always tell the truth, I never cheat on my wife and then what do you do? The opposite, in the next possible moment.

You cannot trust anybody and there is no need to trust. Everything is possible. Fantastic! Every moment. Behind every corner, there wait infinite directions.

Q: Mind blowing!

K: Yeah. The mind is blowing. [Laughter] The answer is blowing in the wind. Everyone is puzzled by That, if we're one puzzle then why does everyone wake up in a different story? There is no one waking up in anybody. It's just energy becoming active in an experience of a body. There is no one waking up and there is no one born in a body. It's not your body, it's just an experience of a body. Just one camera position looking at the scenery. That's all!

But you're not the camera, it's like a tool. You have two eyes but That what is looking through the eyes, has no eyes. The eyes are just tools of perception. But perception is with and without eyes – what never needs eyes. That's why they call it the third eye, which is looking through the eyes but never needs any eyes. There are so many different tools of perception.

Q [Another visitor]: In my case, why don't I wake up in someone else?

K: You actually do everyday. You wake up everywhere – especially you. [Laughter] But as there is no connection to anything, because there is no two, you cannot experience what happens in the other person. Because there is no connection – no two. The energy here and the energy there are not different, but there is no connection. There is no wire you can communicate with.

In the absolute dream, there is absolute separation, otherwise it would not work. To have this individual experience, really individual, you have to be disconnected from everything. Otherwise it doesn't work. How otherwise can you have a sip of water or something and experience it? I just say it is as it is. One doesn't have to know why and how it works.

So, even to know all the mechanics, doesn't give you an advantage. Just see That what wakes up in this body is – with and without the body – what-it-is. And if That what is waking up in this body, is with and without what-it-is, it's true in every case. There is no one waking up in anybody. It's all like puppets on the string of existence and existence plays everyone – call it consciousness, call it whatever.

Q [Another visitor]: In dreams there is much more fluidity of identity...

K: You can meet multiple personalities there. From one second to another, infinite personalities show up.

Q: I mean in night dreams there is a degree of not being fixed on one body and you can meet two or three personalities and things like that...

K: Sometimes I meet that kind of people here too. [Laughter] Sometimes it's strange when I look at someone, I see many faces. I see the whole lineage of whatever this body comes from. All the ancestors shining through and they're shining through everyone. Sometimes you see it and sometimes not. Sometimes it's obvious and sometimes it's fixed.

Every figure is like a sculpture coming from all the sculptures before. It's just a result of all the sculptures that were before in another incarnation. This is a result of all what was there before. You can go back to Adam and Eve, but you cannot find the end of it. For me, you see one sculpture and you go back and back and what you see is this one again. It's like chicken and the egg. You can never say what was first. Is the chicken the kid of the egg or the egg the kid of the chicken? What comes first?

For me both came together. There was never any mother of a

child. You have a mother of a child, then the mother is actually caring about her mother. Because what you care about is your future which is your past. You will be the child of your child and the child cares about the child. Who is the mother? Who is the child? Who created who? You can never figure out.

For me, it's all a reaction of that action which is called life. Reaction, reaction, reaction. The next reaction ends up in this reaction. So, it's all already here – infinitely repeating itself. Not even repeating itself, it never goes and never comes – this moment.

Q: But hasn't there been a tendency over historical times for the experience of separation to get much more pronounced? For example people in tribal society are much more identified with the tribe than those who live as individuals...

K: They don't care if someone dies, because no one gets lost. It happens, that's one way of existence experiencing itself – in a more oneness tribe. Now we're in the western world, more individual separated one. It's just one play of existence, in a different way and none of them is better. That is part of separation and this is part of separation. Even oneness is part of separation. All experiences, realization and realization can only happen in separation. In an imaginary separation.

So, the imaginary separation demands that there is oneness – which is separate from separation. So, even oneness is separate from separation. The one and two come together. Oneness and two-ness are made out of the same metal. If one is there, then the other one is there. You can only realize yourself in separation. What can you do? You will never realize what is realizing itself and whatever you realize, you realize yourself in lies.

You can never know yourself and whatever you can know, is part of realization. It's not different from you, but it's not part of what-you-are – it's false. Ramana called it false, I call it shit – just two different words.

Q: So That what is realizing itself, is false?

K: No. That what is realizing itself, you can call reality. But reality can never know reality because there are no two realities and for knowing, it needs two.

Q: But why would it want to realize itself in the first place?

K: It has to! Look, it did! There was a divine accident. Buddha called it the divine accident – out of the blue. There was not even reality wanting it – just happened. Not out of need, for sure not. It doesn't need it, but shit happens. That's why it's called shit happens. Not because reality was alone up there and God was alone and then he created his children so that he is not alone. Ha, Ha Ha!

No! It was an accident. It's like the condom exploded. [Laughter] Imagine God is cumming, what condom can hold what comes out of that? [Laughter] It's an ecstatic waking up – God is cumming – watch out!

Q: I'm reading about Mehar *Baba*...

K: The one who never spoke until the last ten minutes of his life. [Laughter] He promised that he will never speak again because he said the moment I speak again, there will be an energetic explosion and every one will be enlightened. That would be too much for humanity. But in the last ten minutes he started to talk because he had to go to the hospital and the taxi was late. He sat there and yelled – 'Where is my taxi?' And that was the explosion of the world...

Q: Do you just make up these stories? [Laughter]

K: We have a lady from India. Did I make it up?

Q [Indian lady]: No!

K: It's true. That's why I go to India because I like the stories of the *Gurus* who give so many promises and can never keep it. I like all the *Gurus*. There's another one in Tiruvannamalai, called Nannagaru. He's very famous in south India, thousands of ladies go to him. He always said Shakespeare must be realized. It had to be a realized guy who wrote all those stories. Then he went to London to the house where Shakespeare was born. He went to the desk – Oh yes, this is the desk of an enlightened man. [Laughter] Yes, I feel it, there was enlightenment sitting here and meditating. Yes! Yes! Then went to toilet – Yes, there were enlightened poops here! [Laughter] Then he went out to the gardener and he said – Isn't it a nice house and there's such a nice energy in the house of Shakespeare. The gardener replied, Shakespeare? That is the house of his mother. The house of Shakespeare is that one. [Laughter] And then he was into the taxi and never seen again.

So, what did Mehar *Baba* say? [Laughter]

Q: He also called it the divine accident...

K: I like the divine accident more because it points to the helplessness of existence. It's not by any intention. There's no intention in existence – there was never, is never and will never be any intention of existence. So, all of that is an accident. What to do? You cannot find any guilty guy, not even God. An accident cannot be avoided – that's all. Who's guilty? There was never any guilt in anything.

But if it's the divine poem, then you can always say – Who is this fucker who made this poem? Kill him right away. If this is the poem, it's really a bad one.

Q: It does occur to me that it could be improved...

K: Yeah! [Laughter] You see, if you call it a poem you always say it could be done better – this bloody poem. But if it's a divine accident – it's peace. Then there's no one to blame for anything. Neither God or yourself. All of this is an accident. An accident just points to the fact that no one ever wanted it. No one could ever control anything. Not even God can control his realization. For control, it needs two.

If reality would be different from the realization, then reality could control realization. But reality in nature is realization. There is no two and how can That what is the nature control nature? And where is the need for it? So, what to do?

This is entertainment, that's the beauty of it. It's just

entertainment because there is nothing to gain by it. It doesn't make you more or less or the accident doesn't get solved. You don't have to fix the car.

Yeah, my dear accidents. Some believe out of which mother they would come out and when! [Asking a visitor] Did you know?

Q [Another visitor]: I don't know...

K: So you're an accident. And no one is insured.

Q [Another visitor]: When consciousness is playing with itself...

K: It's imagining to.

Q: It's totally impotent...

K: It cannot decide how to play.

Q: But somehow you and Buddha claim that everything is suffering...

K: I don't claim that, I just see it. Imagine I would claim suffering!

Q: Buddha says this suffering will never end...

K: It's not actually suffering, it's a misinterpretation. It's actually experience of discomfort.

Q: But somehow some aspects can realize...

K: What aspect can realize?

Q: Buddha realized that there's only suffering and it will never stop...

K: The discomfort will never stop because the realization will never stop. And realization will always be in the discomfortable experience of separation.

Q: But there must be somewhere a possibility that the whole game stops. Why does it have to be discomfortable? Why cannot one play this game as comfortable?

K: It's still the discomfort of separation. When you play a

comfortable game, you want to make it oneness which is part of separation.

Q: As you say there is a total block in which pictures come, but the seer is separate from the picture, but the perception is always...

K: There is discomfort but no one is in that discomfort. So, what's the problem?

Q: But the normal people...

K: The normal people? Now you're in a hospital again.

Q: Is accident same as mistake?

K: Yeah. It's a me-steak. That's the nature of a mistake. You take yourself as a steak – it's a me-steak. Then something is at stake because if you're a steak then something is at stake. Shit! I like English. Such a funny language.

It's a mistake – you take yourself as something you're not. That's the accident. So, you get identified with this steak. That's called me-steak. Then she asks, isn't it possible that some mistakes can be happy?

Q: But there must be something...

K: Fiction!

Q: You say it's not possible, I say it's possible...

K: Stay there but leave me alone. Just go, where you think it's better. She cannot see that she creates separation from this and that. She just plays with concepts and all the concepts are imaginary ideas and fiction there will always be discomfort in all the fiction and all the images. It doesn't matter how they are – it's all discomfort. Compared to the comfort of absence of what-you-are, there is no one who has any idea of how it has to be. All, even the most beautiful what you can imagine to be, is discomfort. All of that is discomfort. Absolutely completely.

The best is this knowledge. Compared to this knowledge, which is knowledge, all you can know – the whole universe. Whatever can be known in the bloody universe – is ignorance. Knowledge cannot be reached. The same is with happiness. Whatever you can experience in this world is discomfort – compared to the happiness of what-you-are because there is no one who needs it.

All the fulfillment of the whole universe, all the orgasms together, whatever all the girls and boys had together in the whole existence, compared to That ecstasy of what-you-are – is a piece of shit and I mean it. What-you-are is uncomparable. Your nature is uncomparable to imaginary so-called peace or happiness or knowledge or knowing or not knowing or all your imaginary... [blowing in the wind]

Otherwise why are you longing for That what-you-are? Because you already know That's the only thing what can fulfill you – to be what-you-are and nothing else. Otherwise, you would not have already turned to That what-you-are. Otherwise you would still go to the world and the discos, fucking around the clock. [Laughter] Everyone here already tried all those possibilities, going around with all the sex *gurus* and six *gurus* and artificial *gurus* and *dikshas* and *darshans* and peaceful presences and you all have to leave again – that peaceful presence of a peaceful *guru* – pee-is-full. The bladder is full, so pee where-you-are. [Laughter]

Any other idea of where there should be happiness? It's all 'should' – rubbish.

Q: So, your true nature is when you don't know yourself, you are the Self...

K: I would not call it true nature. I would just call it That what-you-are. Because true nature makes it important again.

Q: It's almost like a trance because when you're in trance you forget yourself...

K: Yeah. It's like a trance of the absence. It's like you go to a bar and you drink yourself to the absence and then you're fine. You don't know who you are anymore. That's called bar meditation. [Laughter] It's the most famous meditation in the whole world. You see it everywhere.

Q: That and watching soccer...

K: Yeah. Drinking and watching soccer has double benefit. You have a reason to drink and you have company of drinking.

Q: And the next morning you forget...

K: No. You have a hangover. You know you have a hangover but you can always drink again. Then you become an alcoholic – just trying to have comfort all the time. That makes you an alcoholic.

They even asked Ramana – Can I reach my natural state with drugs? He replied – Yes, temporarily, but you always come back in this discomfort. Then you want to stop it again by drugs and sex and rock n' roll and temporarily maybe you even get to that, but only temporarily. You have to be what-you-are in the presence of discomfort and in the absence of discomfort. So, what to do?

And the hangover after the so-called artificial drugs is quite bad.

Q [Another visitor]: Same here... [Laughter]

K: Now he tells me again that you are my drug. I'm your push-up, the guy who sells you the drug, but you don't pay enough. I always tell people – If you pay more, I could give you more. [Laughter]

Consciousness has many ways, many drugs, many possibilities, many techniques to shift between the presence and the absence. So, heaven and hell will always be there. You always shift between – by whatever technique and for sure, your most common wish is to remain in heaven forever. That you call enlightenment. You think if you're enlightened, you abide in absence and then you will be happy forever in that comfort zone of absence. This is the idea about enlightenment or realization. You establish yourself in the absence. Then the presence is only like fleeting shadows in front of you but no one is concerned what is happening or not. That would be the ideal position.

But you cannot. You're always stupid enough to fall in love with what is there and you go back to business. No one can remain forever in That so-called *samadhi* of absence.

Q [Another visitor]: And how can the root thought of 'I Amness' be eradicated?

K: You cannot and that is annihilating it totally because you are what-you-are, with and without it. That is out-rooting the idea that you can ever get rid of what-you-are. Because you are That. You realize yourself first as 'I' and then the 'I Am' and then whatever comes after that. That is what-you-are. That is out-rooting the idea that something has to be out-rooted for you to be what-you-are. The 'me' is only the idea that something has to go for the 'me' to be what the 'me' is.

This idea gets out-rooted that something has to be out-rooted to be what-you-are. That is the devotion of devotion or renunciation of renunciation. You renounce the renouncer by just being what-you-are. That is out-rooting the idea that you can ever leave yourself. As you are That reality, which has to always realize itself – whether you like it or not, you're just That what is the helplessness itself which has to realize itself whether you like it or not. With all likes and dislikes, all beauty and ugliness and all what you can imagine.

And you have to always realize yourself as an imagination and first of the imagination is – that first one who is imagining. It is already part of the imagination, but who is imagining the one who is imagining? You cannot find and That never needs anything, but still it cannot stop realizing itself.

So, the next sip of coffee, the next experience will be there – if you like it or not.

Q [Another visitor]: And all of that is a result of fear?

K: No. There is no fear. For what-you-are, there was never any fear. But if you're crazy enough to shift to the first – that you're the creator and then you're different from creation, all that is experience of fear. But from what-you-are, there's not even an experience. You're just That what is the experiencer, experiencing what is experienced. That cannot get out of what-it-is.

You're the infinite traveler between all the seven possibilities of realizing yourself. From all personal point of views, from all impersonal, all beyond views, you have to realize yourself.

You fear that you cannot take it, that it will not stop. But when you are what-you-are, it's more than easy. It's your nature to be That and there is no one who can fear himself.

But you fear that you cannot take it. You think, I'd rather stay here where something happens than there where nothing happens. So, you fear more the boredom of that nothing ever happens, That you cannot take it. And by fearing that there's nothing ever happening, you better stay here – in that hell of relative pain. It's bullshit!

It still continues. The whole thing continues. The movie goes on, you cannot miss anything. You cannot miss yourself. This will be forever, your infinite movie. There's nothing to fear. The next will be the next and you will be entertained by what-you-are forever.

Q: Yeah but fear is still there...

K: Yeah, it's part of the experiences, but who wants it? You see, you cannot find the owner. So, who cares? A fictive ownership, a fictive owner, cares about a fictive fear. Fiction! And then you become a scientist and then it all becomes a science fiction. A seeker is like a scientist who wants to discover himself – like a little Columbus. [Mocking] For the first time the self was discovered by me. Then being a realized one sitting there – I've realized my true nature. As if it's something new or something fresh – Me! There were no aboriginals before! Because of 'me', I know now that it exists. There was no self before I realized myself. Isn't it crazy?

I realized 'my' self. What does that mean? An asshole realized to be an asshole? Okay. Let him have his realization.

Q: You said that the one we imagine is already imagined...

K: Yeah. The absolute seer is imagining a relative seer. So, out of the absolute seer, the *Parabrahman*, he imagines *brahman*. And already *brahman* is an imagination of *Parabrahman* and only the *Parabrahman* is real. The *Parabrahman* not knowing reality and that's the nature of reality. For reality, there is no reality. There is not even an idea of reality and only in unreal, there are ideas of reality – of real and unreal. In reality, there is no such thing as real or unreal. It doesn't even know itself.

So, *Parabrahman* is *brahman* not knowing itself. In its absolute nature. But the moment he knows himself, he becomes relative – relative creator, creating relative ideas of imaginary events and worlds and universes.

Q: Is the thinking same as imagining?

K: The question is who is thinking the thinker? You cannot find that bastard and if you want to stop thinking, you know that I have some techniques. Try to think in Mongolian. You cannot even think 'I' in Mongolian. Instant stop! Try! Blank – totally blank. There is no 'me', there's no 'I', there are no others in Mongolian. You don't even have a name. But after a while, you may learn Mongolian and then you're in the same shit.

There is not even a memory if you cannot speak the language. It's amazing. You have to pronounce what you remember. You have to pronounce a tree to see a tree. If you would not know English, you would not know what is a tree. This would all be – you would not know what it is. Like a baby – brmmm, brmmm, brmmm...

Q [Another visitor]: Is direct perception without symbols and representations?

K: No. It's just different – not direct. There is no direct experience.

Q: In psychology they make a difference between...

K: Psych-chology. They always make differences – Gestalt therapy. Wonderful! It's all working on the side-effects – you know that.

Q: So, no direct perception?

K: How can that happen? What is direct and what is indirect? You must know. What is in psychology direct and indirect perception?

Q: Direct perception is perceiving like a baby without a language...

K: Then there is no perceiver and nothing to perceive. How can that be direct? There is no direction in it. Only when there is indirect, there is direct and in baby there is neither – neither direct or indirect. Otherwise from a position of an indirect perception, you have an imaginary idea of direct perception. From now on, it's all imaginary. It was always imaginary. Even the baby has an imaginary non-perception.

Q: Non-perception?

K: Experiencing no images is still – non-perception. It's still different from perception. Perceiving the absence and perceiving the presence is different – it needs a presence of one. That's too late. It needs a presence of awareness and it's already too late. God is aware to be and then he has a child consciousness and then a grown-up consciousness. The one who has a language to describe what-he-is and an absence of describing of what-he-is. But there is no advantage for a baby.

Q: So, the nature of perception is what?

K: No one will ever know. You will never know – but That is what-you-are. The nature of perception is That perception cannot perceive perception. And whatever the perception is perceiving – especially the perceiver – cannot be That what is perception. That's why they say That perception is closest to That what-you-are – the eye of God. But the eye of God is not God.

So, perception is the closest you can come to That, what is your nature. So, your nature is – whatever is perception, cannot perceive itself – because there's no second. And from there on it becomes like, you perceive an image of a perceiver, perceiving what can be perceived.

Q: Is there already consciousness in perception?

K: Who needs to know?

Q: I have to admit – 'me'...

K: Yeah. That what is there, doesn't need to know what-it-is. Now you want to put it in that mind frame of consciousness – neither. Neither there-is or there-is-not. You can say there's an absolute potential of all possible – what you can call consciousness – the dream or realization of reality. But you cannot call reality, consciousness. You can call it, but then it's the same bullshit as everything.

You don't need to call it anything. You just call it Self, just to make it... You can call it God, but no word fits. Then you come back to the baby. Does the baby know the word 'consciousness'? And does it need to know what-it-is? It needs the tits of his mother – that's all. It's still needy – so it cannot be the Self. It needs something to survive as you now as a grown-up mind need some concepts of survival – of future and past.

Whatever is depending and needs something from something, cannot be the Absolute. It has to be an imaginary concept, an imaginary – fiction, who needs another fiction of survival and presence. So, what to do? So, everyone looks for a way out, but it's no where to be found. Life is hard, makes you tired.

Q [Another visitor]: Is fear another aspect of life loving this dream?

K: Yeah. Because when you're a lover and you have a beloved, you fear that something can happen to your beloved. Then there's fear. You always try to avoid bad things. The moment you wake up, there's always this trinity – the lover, the loving and the beloved.

Then you care about your beloved and then you fear that something may happen to it, what you don't like.

Q: Is that okay instead of loving?

K: You love but now you hate that you love your beloved – you want to get rid of it. It feels like a prison.

Q: Is the Beloved this phantom?

K: This body – everything – whatever is next. Sometimes its your body, or spirit or awareness. It starts with the awareness, it's already your beloved, your awareness, your 'I Amness', your body, your family, your next whatever, your community, your universe. The love starts with awareness. So, you're awareness, that what is closest to you. Your consciousness, your so-called spirit. You have many beloveds – many levels of love.

Q: I don't believe in soul anymore...

K: Then you're in love with that absence of a soul. It doesn't make any difference. Maybe you would be surprised one day that suddenly you have a soul. [Laughter] You go to your toilet and suddenly your soul is next to you. [Laughter]

Q: Some teachers speak about the reality as ultimate intimacy...

K: They say it's closer than your eye-sight and closer than your soul and closer than your awareness. It's an absolute intimacy with what-you-are in which nothing can be more intimate as being what-you-are. There is no distance, that's called absolute intimate, by being That what-you-are. There is no distance, no possibility of distance. That's called being absolute intimate with yourself. There is no close or away from it. So, you can never lose that intimacy.

Q: In absence do we have that intimacy?

K: In absence, as you are That absence, it cannot take That absolute experience away of what-you-are. This is an absolute intimate experience – just-to-be That absolute experience which is in the absence and in the presence. Which you cannot lose. Everything else you can lose. But this absolute intimate – absolute whatever-it-is – call it Heart. The core – to be the core, not having a core. That's the absolute intimate presence.

Q: It's a bit heavy today...

K: Sounds good. The heavy feeling is you're fed up with everything and then you already turn your attention to That what is – what-you-are and everything becomes too much. Then you get angry that you still have to drive, you still have to breathe, you don't like it anymore. You really want to go. You're fed up with everything. You're even fed up by being fed up. [Laughter] All too much – from the beginning. Even getting up in the morning, having a bladder and having to go to the toilet. Doing your make-up... Oh shit!

No one believes me when I say from the basic, there's an unconditional hate that you have to-be. You hate every fucking moment. You take drugs so that you can just take it. You marry someone. You have boyfriends and girlfriends, just that you can take to be alive. Because you hate every fucking moment. If I say it – I mean it. You need all the little things to make it bearable. Otherwise this suicide tendency that you want to get rid of it, is permanent. You meditate – just to meditate it away. You want to get rid of this 'me', this presence, moment by moment. You even sit in the sunset and think that maybe sunset takes me away with it. [Laughter] Take me – I'm fed up.

Q [Another visitor]: For what reason does God play this game?

K: Didn't you listen? [Laughter] Do I have to start again? What did I say ninety minutes ago? For half and hour I was explaining the divine accident and now comes Shalaba. [Laughter] It's like play it again Sam.

Q: I mean it...

K: Why not? If you don't want it anymore, kill yourself, but don't be so angry with us. [Laughter]

Q: It's only with you...

K: You're angry with me, I know. They think, I can take it. All the anger, they put on me. Why does this fucking God even does this to me? [Laughter] Why do I have to exist? I talked about God is angry with himself. Look at Shalaba, she's angry about herself. Why did I do that to me? Fuck me. You should run around with a T-shirt – Fuck me and everyone else – signed Shalaba [Laughter]

Q: In a way, now I'm fed up...

K: She complains about she only takes herself as fucked. But she cannot imagine that she's the fucker, the fucking and the fucked. Now she experiences herself as fucked and that she's fed up, because she's fucked. That's the third[middle] finger, the personal finger. I'm fed up, but you're That fucking and the fucker.

Q: But I'm fed up with this one [closing her fist]...

K: That you cannot.

Q: If this one [closing her fist] is creating all the three – it's stupid... [Laughter]

K: But that's what I told you. When it's absent it's total knowledge and when it opens up, it's absolute stupid. Slowly you believe me.

Q [Another visitor]: It's just that there is more anger here...

K: That's good. Let is out baby. It's not good – but it's fun. I like angry people.

Q: Usually I'm not so angry...

K: Because now it gets more obvious that you cannot get out of it – that there's no way out and that makes you very angry. It's burning like hell. It's called the holocaust of the me.

Q: We're playing here, pretending...

K: Yeah. Generally you try to do something else, take it easy. Have a glass of wine or talk about the bloody tourists standing around and no one needs them.

But here you're confronted. This is a concentration camp. This is a concentration camp – you know that. If you concentrate on That what-you-are, the nature shows itself as a never ending story of 'I' and for that phantom, it becomes very angry. It gets angry and then self-pity – poor me – and all what comes with it. Because anger and self-pity come together. Why did that guy do it? Fuck you all. Maybe you're confronted that there was never anything you controlled and your impotence becomes obvious. Then you become angry.

You know that. When people become old, they have less energy and they become really angry – if they get helpless, if they cannot drive the car anymore. My father gets the car out of a garage and bumps into someone and starts shouting – Why did you park your car there? You bloody asshole. It was not me – it was you. Always blaming someone else.

What do I say? I always say, it was bad, it is bad and it will be bad – and there's no way out. It's bad.

Q: I prefer to know That truth, whether it's beautiful or not...

K: That's why in Taoism they say – beautiful words are not real and the reality is never beautiful. It shows you the ocean of pain which you cannot avoid. You have to be what-you-are in the presence of the ocean of pain, because that is compassion. This ocean is an ocean of pain and ocean of humanity and ocean of existence, is existence of pain – and you cannot stop it. It will always be there. This is the way you realize yourself – in the ocean of discomfort, dislike. There will never be an end of it.

As absolute is your comfort, as absolute is your discomfort. As absolute your knowledge, as absolute is your ignorance. You can only realize yourself in ignorance, in discomfort. This is like *Yudhistara* in Mahabharata, Krishna puts him into hell and asks – Can you take it? And he was lucky enough that there was no tendency of avoidance left in it. In that instant his reaction was – Okay, may it be as it is. You are That what is realizing itself, so how can you suffer about yourself? So there was never any sufferer.

There is no possibility of a sufferer but there still is an experience of discomfort, but no one has this experience.

Q [Another visitor]: But why sometimes we see it in the other way? One day you see things in this way and the other day you think it's fantastic...

K: Why do you ask me? [Laughter] I have no idea why are you so different everyday. [Laughter]

Q [Another visitor]: She's a Gemini...

K: Because you're a Gemini. [Laughter] Why should I know why she is so flippy-floppy. [Laughter] For me it's always bad, moment by moment. It's always bad, bad, bad – very bad.

Q: But you have a better body...

[Group laughter]

K: [Laughing] You be quiet, you're as bad as myself. If you would be in this body, you could talk. I cannot find what is not fun and I cannot find what is not bad. It's really bad fun and you're so bad. Whatever you are, you're bad. How can you do that to yourself? You're so bad.[Laughter] If God is so bad, I don't go to heaven – not me. Dear God, I don't want to know you and you don't exist for me anymore. I'm fed up. That's the biggest federation – the fed-up federation.

Q [Another visitor]: How can a phantom have a soul or something like that?

K: Imagine! It's imagining, as you imagine to have a body. How can you have a body? You imagine to have hair. You imagine that you have a hair dresser. [Laughter] That's quite imaginary.

What cannot be imagined? In dream everything is possible. In dream there are souls, there are imaginary masters and disciples. Whatever can be – can be imagined. It's an absolute imagination of That what is not an image. So, That what is not an image, That what neither exist or doesn't exist, is imagining itself in all possible – whatever can be imagined. It cannot imagine itself only in one part. If it starts imagining itself, it has to imagine itself in all possible ways. It cannot just have the comfortable parts. That is what you want and she wants and everyone wants. Just having one part and not the other one. I resist the bad one and only want to have the good one. I only want to feel good. I don't want to feel any pain, no disease, I don't want to age, I don't want to die, I want to be enlightened forever but not have a body. I want to be space-like, I want to be ecstatic moment-by-moment. [Laughter] I want to have an orgasm which never ends. [Laughter] Even if I never had one, I want to have that I could have had. [Laughter] My imaginary one!

Q: Earlier I was agnostic...

K: I like the Gnostics and I like the agnostics.

Q: Then I started to believe in reincarnation and now I don't believe in anything. But people in my surroundings still believe in soul and reincarnation...

K: That story is over.

Q: Everything is over...

K: Not everything, but that story is over. Life will not be over, that story is over. Then comes another imaginary story.

Q: But this phantom doesn't believe...

K: Yeah, can happen. Now you believe that you don't believe.

Q: But even if another story begins, I will not remember that in previous...

K: You never know. [Laughter] Imagine, the Dalai Lama – fifteen times now. He always remembers his things and now he's really fed up. Next he wants to be reincarnated as a house wife in America. [Laughter] Shaking Martini's and having more time for meditation. Because as a Dalai Lama, he has no time to meditate. As a housewife in America you have plenty of time and then he meditates and he thinks he can stop the wheel of reincarnation. Because he's really fed up, because he remembers all that shit.

But if you don't remember in the next, you maybe have a boyfriend who's a reincarnation master who remembers you. [Laughter] That's bad luck. I had this experience. I had a girlfriend for one year, she was a reincarnation master. Every time I went to bed, I had these bloody experiences of all what was there before. I didn't ask for it but in her presence, it just came naturally.

Q: How was it?

K: It was fun. I just saw my television. [Laughter] I didn't go so far, but it was quite entertaining. Being a Sufi in Persia or a being a Mexican-Indian digging in a mine.

Q: If someone tells me that, I'd run away. My heart gets blocked when I think like that...

K: You're now everything. What is the problem of having all the things before? You're everything.

Q: If a boy friend like that comes, I'd run away...

K: Yeah, but if the love is big enough, you will take the shit. [Laughter]

Q: I don't think that would happen...

K: I would not say that, love can come. I don't want to put a future on you that you don't like. [Laughter] But just-in-case, but what would be the difference, if that happens? Would it make you more or less?

Q: No...

K: So, it may happen or not. The worst case can happen. What would be the problem? And the worst case would be that it would never stop – the whole holocaust.

Q: I see what you say, that it may come. I even love the idea of never ending story...

K: Yeah. There's peace. What's best is, in That peace never anything happened and nothing can come and nothing can go. So, this is eternal. What can be better?

Q: But this story, this phantom cannot imagine...

K: If there's natural resistance, then there's no problem with it. But what's resistance one day, can be broken tomorrow. If totality wants it, it breaks it – as nothing and then he would never be sure of anything. No one knows how he would react to whatever happens tomorrow or in the future.

Q: Every time I tried to confirm my life, it didn't work, at work, at relationships. All my plans were completely defeated and then it was okay...

K: Look at all these people – it's all bad, but they're all relaxed in it. It would really be bad if you think something could be different. But if it was bad, it is bad and it will be bad – who cares? The next boyfriend is as bad as the one before. It's different bad, but it was bad.

But for me it's such a relaxation. You know it was bad, it is bad and it will be bad. So what? Shit, shit, shit. What's the problem? If you really don't expect that the next shit will be good shit, who cares?

Q [Another visitor]: What if it gets worse?

K: It's bigger shit. Now you have a 'me' and then you have a 'bigger me'. Then they all get silly here. That's the sign when something goes really bad, they get silly. It's like – okay, why not? Then the nonsense makes more sense than all the sense of the world. That's called entertainment – absolute non-sense. Then the sixth sense of humor comes out, which is maybe your true nature. Because you know that only you can do things like that to you, as no one else could do to you. [Laughter]

She's right. No one else can be as bad to you, as you can be bad to yourself. No one else can have such a sadistic, masochistic relationship with you as you have with yourself. No one else would do the things to you that way. Without any mercy, there is no mercy to yourself – never. You are That grace that knows no mercy and that never shows mercy to itself. Because you know nothing can happen to you. By instinct, by intuition, you know nothing will ever happen to you. So, you can do the worst thing what you cannot even imagine. [Laughter]

And then at the end you laugh, ha, ha, ha – nothing ever happened. Then out of the ashes, the phoenix arises – ha, ha, ha, look at me. All that bullshit happened and all that madness and all that disaster and all that pain. Ha! Here I am again! After all that pain!

You are the beast, who always wakes up again as a beast. You cannot be burnt down by your own fire – that's the whole story – but you try.

Q [Another visitor]: And try and try...

K: Mick Jagger – I can't get no, but I try. In all possible ways, to get what I don't need. I try to get what I don't need and I try really hard! And I give it to me – that what I never needed. [Laughter] And I will beat myself up for that.

So, my dear friends – pain in the ass. [Laughter] Where else you can talk to yourself like that? It's all a pain in the ass. Shit! That I have an ass. Shit – because I have an ass. I have to shit – shit! Why do I have an asshole? Shit! [Laughter]

Okay! Thank you for going [Laughter]

June 11, 2012. Evening Talk.
Mallorca, Spain

May it be as it is – that is instant fulfillment

Q: When a phantom is seen as a phantom, is that still a phantom?

K: Yeah. But it's not like being seen as a phantom. That would be a different phantom who sees it as a phantom. Then there are two phantoms.

Q: It's not like the Absolute sees the phantom?

K: No. The Absolute is inspite of the phantom – with and without the phantom. But it never sees the phantom. The Absolute is experiencing itself as a phantom, which means that the Absolute is experiencing it. But the Absolute is with the experience what-it-is and without the experience what-it-is. So, it never sees a phantom because then there would be two phantoms.

God is experiencing himself as God. But the experience of God is not the nature of God. So, the experience of God is a phantom experience – like an imagination of God. It's an image of God, not the nature of God. The phantom is an image, a mask of God, but not the nature of God. If there would be a phantom who sees a phantom as a phantom, that would be a schizophrenic phantom.

Q: Once the relative goes...

K: How can it go? Already when you say 'once', that implies a special moment, a special absence or something disappears or something is seen as something. All of that is a relative realization. And out of the relative realization come results or consequences. But not from the Absolute experiencing itself as a phantom or God experiencing itself as God. There is no consequence in it – by being what-he-is, which is with and without that experience. That never calls anything as phantom. It's just That what-is with and without.

So, there is no consequence and there is no 'one' who talks about – after that experience, I am different. That's all fairy tales. Being what-you-are never needs any consequence, change, better life or now I am living the truth bullshit. All what people say afterwards, is a relative realization claiming that now they know their true nature and now it's a different story. Never!

Q [Another visitor]: But forty years ago, you didn't speak like that...

K: And you didn't fart like this!

Q: I don't know...

K: You see, even I don't know. How can you say how I spoke?

Q: I didn't hear but you probably didn't speak like this...

K: I spoke like this. I spoke the same bullshit that I speak now. There is no difference.

Q: What was your point on you marveling on the pig getting killed...

K: It was all bullshit. You never listen to me.

Q: I try my best...

K: No. You try to avoid listening. You try to understand, and that is trying to avoid listening. If you would listen, you would not even have a question anymore. You try to understand and that is trying to avoid – That. You want to make it 'your' understanding. By that you take yourself as special and by that you are ignorant.

Now you even want to survive by 'I must be special like you are special'. That's your survival system.

[Visitor shakes head in disagreement]

Don't shake your head, I know you. I see you. Everyone is like that, it's not him alone. Trying to understand is avoiding listening because there is hearing. And you are here because you want to understand and you want to fit something together. You want to put things together, you want to have an understanding, you want to make a story out of it. Otherwise how could he say that forty years ago you spoke differently? He wants to make a story out of it by claiming that I am now different than forty years ago. That is like trying to survive his own story.

What else? And that's a story of the 'me'. What else can it do?

Q: Then what is it for you? Is it a story of 'me-lessness'?

K: Whatever you say now comes from a relative understanding and trying to figure out something. I don't need to understand anything to be what I Am. So, I don't need any understanding at all. But you need understanding.

Q: So, there's a difference...

K: There is a difference but it doesn't make a difference. You play stupid and I don't. But That what plays stupid is not different from that what plays not stupid. You pretend and here there is no pretending – that's all.

Q: So, pretending has ended there?

K: It never started for That what I Am.

Q: Come on!

K: Now you are pretending. [Laughter] Now he wants to make a story again – In your case it stopped.

Q: Yes!

K: No it never stopped. I still pretend to be Karl.

Q: But I am more pretending than you for sure. I pretend more solidly and you are just playing with it...

K: He is a solid player, he plays bridge.

Q [Another visitor]: He plays guitar...

K: No. The guitar plays him.

Q: But normally...

K: Who wants to be normal?

Q: I don't want to be normal...

K: That's because you are normal. Only when you are normal, you don't want to be normal. I have no idea what is normal. So, I don't need to avoid to be normal.

Q: Are you just confirming what I said?

K: That you are normal? To be stupid is normal and not to be stupid is not normal? I say both is stupid.

This is like a ping-pong. But it is That who plays both the sides. No, you can never make me admit that here there is one who realized anything – you know that. You try very hard but no one ever succeeded in making me admit that I ended something.

Q: The one who assumed to be 'solid' – Karl – he's gone now...

K: Who says that? I always say that Karl is fully functioning here and is a bigger asshole than before – day-by-day.

Q: But someone is talking in a different way than everybody else in this room...

K: Lalit knows the same but he just cannot put the words together. [Laughter]

Q [Another visitor]: You have more training...

K: More training? How many excuses does not one need?

Q [Another visitor]: This seems to be the survival system. It's like *gurus* telling you something would happen but nobody knows what should happen...

K: [Mocking] Yeah and they talk about deepest possible despair and out of that there was an explosion.

Q: Yeah and then he also has to be the same way...

K: Yeah and if I cannot talk like him, then I cannot be That. This sounds normal for the phantom but it's totally artificial for what-you-are and there is no bridge. For That what is art, whatever can be said – is artificial. Because That what is art, never needs to express art. And that what needs to express art, is an artist and whatever art he expresses, is artificial. Fishing – selling fish.

Q: But the phantom gets so much food from so-called people...

K: It's like one phantom entered another reference point and feeding someone who's still hungry. One claims that he is not so hungry anymore, feeding someone who claims that he's still hungry. There is a co-dependency, everywhere. It's a blind leading the blind. A blind who has a little glimpse of something, but he doesn't even know from what. Then he talks about the glimpse – I saw the light. And you say – I never saw the light, so he must be very special.

No. I always say, I am the darkness that I cannot see – I can only be. [Mocking] And from darkness I come and to darkness I go and darkness is my underwear. [Laughter] And I am unaware of darkness.

Q [Another visitor]: As I understand it, it doesn't have any criteria – neither internal nor external...

K: Yeah. Having absolutely no idea of what-you-are and what-you-are-not. Don't forget what-you-are-not. You neither know what-you-are and what-you-are-not. That's the absolute absence of any idea. If you know what-you-are-not, you still claim to know what-you-are. No. You neither know what-you-are or what-you-are-not.

Q: You can't even say you are not the phantom?

K: No. When there is the phantom, I am the phantom. When there is no-phantom, I am not the phantom. I can never be not That. This just-is, but I Am with and without. I Am with that experience of a phantom and I Am without that experience of a phantom – that's all. But I Am not the one experiencing the phantom and then being the Reality and saying that I Am the Reality and what I experience is not real. I cannot even say that.

I have absolutely no idea of what is real and is not real. I have absolutely no idea of any Reality or realization. Because first you need to have an idea of reality and then realization and all of that. If you ask me, it's all fucking fiction.

Does *atma* know *atma* when *atma* is *atma*?

Q [Another visitor]: So I Am and I Am not! What about neti-neti? [Laughter]

K: Is she knitting? You still need a pullover? You are afraid that you may freeze without a pullover – sooner or later. You always imagine that winter may come back again and then you need your pullover again.

Q: This was not the question...

K: Yes, that was the question. What about the neti-neti? Can I take the *neti-neti* home? Or shall I forget it right away? What is your neti-neti?

If you ask me, all is a fucking concept. What-you-are never needed any *neti-neti* and that who says *neti-neti* is...

Q: But it was you who always said neti-neti... [Laughter]

K: Now she wants to keep it. When you take the neti-neti, I destroy it. That's the way it goes here. The moment you takes a concept, it's me who destroys it.

Q: I don't want to take it...

K: You took it already.

Q: I didn't want to...

K: But you still took it. Now it sticks to you. I like English. The moment you have a clue, you are glued to that what you have a clue about. It's like Johannes, he has a clue and that's his whole problem. He knows too much, everyone knows too much. It's all too much.

Q [Another visitor]: Does it need to go away?

K: It doesn't need to go away. That's not the point.

Q: I knew too much when I met you and I was not interested in whatever you were saying...

K: And now you are interested?

Q: In a way. But it's not for getting anything...

K: But you want to be happy!

Q: No it is not even that...

K: Of course, you want to be happy and that you call peace. Don't lie now.

Q: It's not that. It's like, rather not be at all...

K: But that's peace.

Q: But there's nobody there anymore...

K: That's your way of peace, that there's no one left for peace. So, it's peace you are looking for. Everyone is looking for peace and the best would be the 'me' is not there who's looking for peace. That would be the peace of 'me' – piss-off 'me'.

Q: There is not even 'me' or anything else...

K: But who needs that? Say it!

Q: The one who is too much here...

K: So, the 'me' needs not to be 'me'.

Q: But it can go now...

K: No one needs your fucking generosity. [Laughter] My 'me' could go now, I don't need it anymore. It's like wanting to fly away. Everyone I meet is like that, there's nothing special about it. Everyone has this idea that without this 'me', I would be better off. So, 'me' – go now, I don't need you anymore. I know that I don't need you, why are you still there?

That's knowing too much. Now I know that I am too much with this 'me', so why this bloody 'me' is still there?

Q: I don't even care if I Am without the 'me'...

K: But you just said that this 'me' can go now and I wouldn't care. So, you know yourself as That who doesn't need any 'me'. Why do you now say something different? Don't play my game! [Laughter]

You know that you take it too fucking serious anyway. There is an importance, a heaviness in it. And that you want to get rid off.

Q: I agree...

K: And you are just listening to these words because they are just light. But they cannot bring you the unbearable lightness of life. They can only talk to that. But Johannes wants to make it 'his' lightness. He would even say that I Am beyond That. I don't even want to have it anymore.

But even not wanting to have it is one too many who doesn't want to have it anymore. The 'me' always wants to have it. What's the problem? He will always try to get it. Let him try. Nothing has to be changed, nothing has to be different for what-you-are. But there's still a subtle idea – that something should be changed, something should be different.

I just sit here and I am wrong even if I care or don't care about it. Caring about wrong is as wrong as not caring about wrong. It's all wrong, wrong, wrong. No one is more wrong than this guy [pointing to himself] here. But there's always a subtle idea that it should be right one day. Then I would write a book about it, as everyone is doing. The moment of 'rightness'. [Laughter]

You know when I started talking, I resisted very hard to sit somewhere and talk about this thing. But look at me – resistance is futile. If I have to talk anyway... and you have to listen...

Q [Another visitor]: We are in the same boat...

K: We are the boat! That's absolutely not to know where-you-are and where-you-are-not. It was always like that, there was never anyone who knew what-he-was and what-he-was-not. What is more natural than that? That's called knowledge. But That what is knowledge, doesn't know any knowledge. The knowledge is that 'you-are' and that is not something you can know. And it is not something that can go now because I don't need you anymore. That knowledge is helplessness. This is the absolute helplessness in its nature – this controllessness.

I am so bad, I like to be bad. I never like to be good, it's much more fun to be bad. [Laughter]

Q [Another visitor]: You can try to be good... [Laughter]

K: That's the devil trying to convince you – Look God you can be good. If you try to be good, you must be bad. So, I better be bad. But she wants me to try to be good, so she's the devil.

Q [Another visitor]: But you must be good because someone sees compassion in your eyes... [Laughter]

K: That's only the devil who sees compassion in my eyes. [Laughter] They want to put me into the hell of compassion. Because if I have compassion in my eyes, she doesn't see compassion in other eyes. So, she makes it special again. Then I am special again and then I am in hell. They try everything. Everyone tries to put me in special position. By saying he's so good and he has so much compassion – that's the worse! Fuck them all and kill them all! Whoever tells me that I'm good and I have compassion in my bloody eyes – watch out! [Laughter]

If you see how the devil works in every bloody sense and way of making you special, because the devil himself needs to be special, he makes you special. So that his hell: can burn forever. [Mocking] But you didn't talk like this forty years ago. Again special! That you can remain as a special asshole you think you are.

Q: Then it doesn't remain special?

K: I'm Absolute special, I tell you. [Laughter] Look how mischievous this asshole devil is. [Joking with a visitor] Look at this devil, he has no hair so that even the horns can grow. [Laughter] It's amazing, in all the possible ways, everyone wants to make the other one special. By making him higher or lower than himself, by making him more compassionate or less compassionate. This can only happen in hell, in differences, in whatever ways you try to find special attributes of someone. Because you want to be special, you make someone else special.

Q [Another visitor]: When I say there is no difference...

K: Everywhere there are differences.

Q: You jump on that too...

K: I jump on everything. I kill whatever you say. That's what you are here for – being killed. Why else are you here? You want to be confirmed in your little understanding or what? I kill you anyway.

Q [Another visitor joking]: How long does it take?

K: Forever! I don't care. [Joking] I have time. If I kill you right away, what would be the point? I cut with a very dumb knife. It doesn't even cut, it's just for fun. I pretend as if I cut. What would be my advantage if I really chopped one's head? Then he would be a special one who doesn't have a head anymore. Would it make any difference? Now he's a special one with head and then he would be a special one without head. I pretend as if I cut. I don't even have a knife in my hand. [Laughter] I pretend as if I have a knife.

Q: And then you say – I kill you all...

K: I kill you all because I have no intention of killing anybody – because I don't know anyone who can be killed. That is killing everyone. But not by killing someone and making him headless – bullshit. I kill you because there is no one here who tries to kill you, because no one needs to kill you. That kills you!

We are talking about the absolute killing. The Absolute never needs anyone to come or to go or to be killed. You are not good enough to be killed – never! You are like a little mouse which is being played with. How fucking important can one be by thinking – existence wants to kill him? As if existence cares if he exists or not. And he's sitting and crying – Come kill me, I am so fed up. And existence laughs – Look at him, another one. He will die anyway. Existence is fucking lazy, it never even moves a finger. You may remain as Johannes forever and no one would care.

Everyone thinks grace needs something to do. Then you read books – Your head is already in the tiger's mouth. But it's a paper tiger. [Laughter] The tiger's mouth is like the destiny of what you believe to be, is already dead. It cannot die further – that's all. You are already in the cemetery of life. Who wants to kill you? Who wants to kill a fucking corpse? Who wants to chop a dead head? You are all dead heads.

But that's the way of killing. You show that existence never needs to kill – to be what-it-is. That kills your idea that something has to be killed. This bloody idea that something has to go – Oh God, oh God! [Joking with a visitor] Are you ready?

Q [Another visitor]: For what? [Laughter]

Q [Another visitor]: That is the only right answer... [Laughter]

K: Every bullet would be too much for you, every word is too much. Is there anyone here who is worth any word? Are you worth even to be talked to? You don't even exist, why should I talk to you? It's amazing, they all want to go and not to exist but they want to listen to me and I should talk to them. [Laughter] Fantastic!

[Mocking] I don't want to be anyone, I don't want to listen at all, but please say something!

Q [Another visitor]: Losing interest in peace, is that peace?

K: No. You are just tired that's all. UG Krishnamurti was once flying on a plane to America and an American was sitting next to him. Americans always ask – What are you doing? Where do you come from? How much money do you make? He asked UG – What is your profession? UG said – I am retired. From what? From retirement! [Laughter] Then the American was quiet for the rest of the flight.

That's like Vashistha pointing out – you retire from retirement because you cannot retire from yourself. You renounce renunciation – by being what-you-are. There will never be any possibility of renouncing anything because renouncing is ignorance. You cannot renounce what-you-are. You devote devotion. What is there that is not you? How can you devote something? Does anything belong to you at all? What can you devote? What can you give?

[Joking] Make your decision. If you say I don't want to exist, I don't talk to you anymore. I should ask this question in the beginning, anyone who says I don't want to exist anymore should not come in. [Laughter]

Q [Another visitor]: I don't feel alive inside...

K: But for that you have many questions. [Laughter] If one would know what he is talking about, then he would not make that statement.

Q: I don't feel 'really alive'...

K: What is really alive? What is your fucking idea of really alive? What is your idea of real life?

Q: When this bloody intellect stops to bother you...

K: I say when this bloody intellect fucks you, that's real life. Because life is the fucker, the fucking and the fucked. And if that fucking ever stops, then you are dead, my dear. [Laughter] But I tell you, you cannot stop fucking yourself – if you like it or not. But you want to experience a real life – where there is no fucker, no fucking and no fucked. [Laughter] What the fuck am I doing here? [Laughter]

[Joking with the visitor] Constantine says, after a few drinks – I am still not drunk. I am still fucking my mind. He thinks the mind is not worth fucking, but the Self he would fuck moment-by-moment. My beloved one, but not my enemy – my 'me'. I want to fuck my beloved, not my enemy. If I fuck my 'me', it's a mind-fuck. And I really want to fuck –my Self! Is that what you want to do? [Laughter] I always fuck with this artificial body. I want to fuck with my real body. And I really want to feel myself – in reality and not with this artificial piece of meat with an artificial brain. I want to be the absolute *lingam* that penetrates itself. [Laughter] I want to swallow myself.

You see, I should be frustrated, and actually I am. I do the best I cannot do and then comes this. [Singing] That's why in the last years Papaji – let's dance. [Laughter]

Q: How can you continue answering these stupid questions?

K: Sport! Like playing cards. You don't play cards to become a millionaire or to really win. It's just that you play cards. Watch out, I may try three months of not talking. But then they threaten me – You would miss us. After a month you would long for our stupid questions and you would long that you answer again for nothing and nothing will come out of it and no one will ever understand what you say and there is no getting it and no one has ever got it anyway. You will miss that. [Laughter] You will miss that someone tells you that compassion comes out of your eyes. You will really miss that someone wants to put you in the same hell as himself. [Laughter]

Q: Real life is one that has no hope...

K: Why? What kind of real life would it be that needs hope to go?

Q: I just repeat the concepts that I read from books...

K: Yeah. It's like a disease, a why-rus(virus) – Why? Why? Why? And now you want to get healthy again because you believe that you are sick. All these ideas of how it has to be and all these masters – kill them all and fuck them all and never listen to them again – if you can. All these fake *gurus* everywhere, including this one [pointing to himself]. It's all fake.

Q: But for me it's not fake. For me you are the best...

K: The best fake. [Laughter] Any idea that you have about how it has to be, is hell. And not having it, is the same hell. You have to realize yourself as hell. There will always be concepts, there will always be – whatever. You can never like that, you can never accept that. It will always be discomfort, what you experience. The moment you experience yourself, you experience yourself in discomfort. The moment you exist, there is a tendency of trying not to exist – instantly. The moment you have this relative existence, you long for the 'real' life. Because by intuition you know that this cannot be it. This discomfort cannot be it – so there is already a seed for that what you call 'real' life.

Then you make all the concepts of truth and how it has to be. By all means you want to get out of that – what is discomfort or so-called separation experience, or whatever you call it. So, what can you do? Never ending story of trying to get out where you are not in – crazy! You want to stop realizing yourself and that's ignorance – as if reality could stop realizing itself. As if existence could retire to that existence which doesn't realize itself. This idea runs in all that – as if you could get out of what-you-are. It's fantastic!

And I can only repeat, there is no way out for you of escaping what-you-are because you are – That. And That what is – That, has many ideas of how it could be and should be. But it still is – what-it-is. And all the should and could and would, can stay or not, it would not make any difference.

It's bad and I like it. [Laughter] No way out! Suffering forever! No one ever made it. No Adyashanti, no Eckhart Tolle, no Ramana, no Jesus. There was never anyone who was realized and realized his true nature – fuck it all! And you will not be the first who would realize his fucking true nature. [Laughter] Who do you think you are? How much arrogant bastard one has to be that he claims that he will be the first who realized his fucking true nature?

There was no Buddha who claimed it, there was no Ramana who claimed it. All of them pointed out that Reality will never be realized by anyone. But you still claim that you can make it. You should be fucked forever in hell, for the idea that you could know your true nature and real life. And you will be fucked forever in hell – for just that idea and wanting to know yourself, you will be punished. That's called the *u-punish-ads* [upanishads].

The moment you want to be special and claim that you are the one who could know your true nature, you are out of your so-called bloody true nature and that is punishment enough. So, you are punished instantly by trying to know your true nature and you should be punished forever. Burn in hell and the fire can never be high enough. [Laughter, clapping]

I have to talk to the devil himself, trying to become God. I may smile at it, but I meant it seriously. [Pointing to a visitor] You will rot in hell forever – especially you. [Laughter]

The question is – Can you take that? For what-you-are, there is nothing to take. You are the hell and you are the devil and there's nothing to burn because you cannot be burnt by yourself. But now you are someone who does not want to be in hell and that burns already.

[A visitor sneezes]

Drop dead you beast! I meant the virus. [Laughter] These are the last two hours, I want to make sure that you don't get anything here.

Q: I don't understand what you say...

K: No. You understand too much.

Q: It's a dead understanding...

K: Every understanding is dead. What is not a dead understanding? Even to understand this is dead. Dead, dead, dead. But still there's a hope of a real understanding.

Q: It's very stupid...

K: The whole humanity lives by that. It seems like it has to be there. That's the way it is.

Q: But in your case, it seems you have no hope...

K: But I'm still sitting here and talking to you. What's the difference?

Q: The difference is that you have no hope and I have hope...

K: I still have a hope that one day you may not understand. [Laughter]

Q [Another visitor]: Instant fulfillment...

K: The instant fulfillment is – may it be as it is. That's already as it is, as stupid as it is. What to do?

Q [Another visitor]: When one tries to understand, one is out of it?

K: No. Knowledge imagines that it has lost knowledge, so it tries to go back and tries to understand what-it-is. It's an imaginary getting out.

Q: Out of what?

K: Out of itself.

Q: By imagining?

K: Of course, you dream to be Rudie now. How can you not? That's an imaginary Rudie, then you are rude. Nothing is being more rude to yourself as imagining yourself to be Rudie, having a body, having a husband, you imagine all of that.

Q: Does it make a difference?

K: Of course, you are missing what-you-are by not being what-you-are.

Q [Another visitor]: But surely understanding has some role to play. If I meet someone next week and he asks him how did the retreat go? [Laughter]

Q [Another visitor]: Tell them you didn't go... [Laughter]

K: What would you say?

Q: If they ask me what you said, I would be in some difficulty...

Q [Another visitor]: Some?

K: It seems to be impossible to repeat what happens. Even I cannot repeat that.

Q: I can buy the tape and listen but then it becomes like I am trying to understand what is being said...

K: First you try, then you exhaust the intention of trying to understand and suddenly you listen and you absolutely don't care about what is being said. There is listening because in listening there is no expectation of understanding.

Q [Another visitor]: And that is better than trying to understand?

K: No. That's meditation, just enjoying the listening and knowing that nothing comes out of it. That's enjoyment and not trying to hear something and trying to understand – that's hard work. That exhausts you.

Q [Another visitor]: Don't you understand what you're saying yourself?

K: No. I don't have to understand That. Why should knowledge need to understand what knowledge never needs? I am so lazy, you cannot imagine. That's the main difference, there is no one here who needs to understand before he says something. It does not come out of any so-called story of understanding which is put together so that people can get it. I have no interest in that.

This is just a ping-pong. I just react to the question. The moment the question is there, I'm never prepared for anything. I don't need to be prepared. I just react in the level of question and destroy both. That's all, because the answer doesn't answer anything. It's just that the question gets destroyed – then comes the next question. [Blowing in the wind] For me this is like the Garden of Eden. Every question is like a flower and there's another flower which is the answer. Both flowers come and go and then there is another flower.

The next is the next, like the sip of coffee or the next question or the next sunset or the next breathing in or the next breathing out. That doesn't need any end. Everyone comes for a final understanding that maybe it will end but for me it never needs to end. It will be the infinite – next and the next. In this Garden of Eden, this paradise of life which is what-you-are. It's not something that needs to be avoided. It's just the next – whatever it is.

And there is no way of escaping that – whatever comes – the next. There is no idea of right or wrong. It is just as it is – just That what-you-are. But the imaginary God always believes in a way out. Then he fights against himself. This is war and then out of this paradise, it becomes a hell because he tries to get out of himself or he wants to control himself. Then he is in hell of himself – of an imaginary war – for peace. Moment by moment, fighting for peace.

There is always peace. There is nothing but peace – call it life. What else is there? And peace is just competing with himself. It's like an Olympic sport. There is no need of winning or gaining something in it – never was. And what is there to do?

Q [Another visitor]: It's like a war...

K: Everything. It's an amusement for what-you-are. There is only amusement, entertainment for what-you-are. But the moment the imaginary 'I' becomes so real that you want to know your real Self, then you become a fake one. Then it becomes seeking, a serious war. You worry about yourself. Then you want to be right because it has to be 'real' life and it has to be this way and you want to have it your way. That's called a seeker and no one is sicker than a seeker.

How can that happen? How can That Absolute even start seeking itself? Look at it – it happens. Then he takes it seriously. It really takes himself important in it. This self pity comes by self importance and then you are really fucked by That. That you feel yourself as special or important or anything. Any moment you believe to be a special asshole – you are fucked by yourself – moment-by-moment. Self guilty from the beginning.

But can you help it? No. You cannot even not do it. It just happened. It's like you are in a hypnotic state – hypnotized by an idea. In India they call it the divine hypnosis, when the Self started to believe in itself. So, he left it's Absolute nature for an idea. Now he tries to get out of the idea – but any moment he tries to get out an idea, it's an idea. Because it tries to confirms by not being an idea, to be an idea.

It's such a mischievous game you play with yourself – wonderful absolute trap. The moment you want to get out of the trap, that is perfect. Even thinking you are out of the trap; you are still in the trap and no one ever made it. When I say there was never any one realized in being realized, just see the beauty in it. As there was never anyone who was realized, there was never anyone in the first place who was not realized. But if there's one who can realize himself, then it confirms all the unrealized ones – instantly. So, the bullshit continues – just by that idea that it could be done, it can be achieved, it can be attained – all of that. This is hell.

The very idea that there was one who made it, that Ramana made it, that there was a Jesus who made it, that there was one who made it, that's hell. None of these made it. I like them all but only because there was no one who made it – never ever. None of these so-called new awakened ones made it. If you cannot make it, fake it. [Laughter]

I don't like Ramana. I like the Self that is pronouncing through that so-called guy Ramana. But I don't have to like Ramana. The Self is ever realized and never needs to realize himself and that who needs to realize itself, is not the Self. It's an imaginary 'I' – an unreal imaginary what?

And that can try forever, it will never realize its nature. Because for that it needs two, if that could be done. That would be hell already. Even the imagination that you can do it, that you need to do it, you are in the hell of imagination. No one of you will ever be happy. [Laughter] That's the best news I can give you. Come on! No one will ever make it to be happy, just see it as there was never anyone who was unhappy – Come on! First show me one who is unhappy and then we can talk about how to make this bloody asshole happy. Show me any one, you just show me what? Ideas, pieces of meat – me-steaks (mistakes). [Laughter]

That's Nisargadatta's Ultimate Medicine – Try to find the unhappy one. You cannot find anyone. Wherever you look, you cannot find yourself – nowhere. As you cannot find the unhappy one – the seeker – who cares? It's not that out of the unhappy one, one becomes happy – No! You cannot find the unhappy one – that's all. Try to find the unrealized one and show it to me. Everyone is claiming and pretending to be one, but when you look for it, it's gone. Where is the asshole that is not realized if you look for it? Corpses unlimited.

It's the last hour, come on! This show has to reach a climax.

Q [Another visitor]: You are doing your best, pearl after a pearl, one bigger than the other one...

K: Imagine I could find anyone worth it. I just give it to myself and even myself doesn't need it. If I could expect someone to get pearls here and be able to use it, I would really be in a piece of shit. There is talking, there is listening but there is no need that something comes out of it – never has.

Q: That's true and never the less…

K: That's the nature of fulfillment that maybe you just are That what never needs to be fulfilled – that's the nature of fulfillment, the nature of Self which never needs to get something out of anything. This is the exercise, what's happening here. There is no need for it and there is no intention in anything. It's just the entertainment of what-you-are. That's fulfillment itself and it will never stop. It was, it is and it will always be the entertainment show of life. Life living life in infinite possibilities and ways and it doesn't even have to enjoy itself.

That's the nature of joy – it never needs to enjoy anything. It can be as much hell as it can be – amusing or not – it's all entertainment. That's the nature of joy, it never needs to enjoy anything – never needed anything. It's never right.

Q: That's the ultimate truth…

K: The ultimate truth is there's no truth – they say. But even that's too much. You need to listen to [Ludwig] Wittgenstein – What you cannot talk about, you should be quiet. This is being quiet – talking like this. You don't have to stay quiet to be quiet. You can say as much as you like and you still will be quiet as if you haven't said a word. Who needs to be quiet to be quiet? It's not sitting somewhere and not saying anything – that's saying too much. That's talking too loud – someone who's not saying something.

But empty words – this is being quiet. That's the silence in the words, the empty words and not sitting somewhere being especially quiet. This is silence. What else is silence?

Q [Another visitor]: So we are in a silent retreat? [Laughter]

K: This is the true nature of a silent retreat and not someone who's quiet and then going to a café where there's no music playing. [Laughter] That's a fake one. It's all fake. Silence never needs anything. Silence is the nature of existence. Talking or not talking doesn't disturb silence. But your personal silence – that's the fuck up. 'I' have to be silent and my silence. Then it becomes very special.

Q [Another visitor]: There is a realization that there are only individual events and not a chain of events...

K: No. There is chain of events. That you can speak, there has to be a chain of events. That you can put the words together, that you could put events together – like a sentence.

Q: They are in my mind...

K: No. I listen to you. They are not in your mind, they are here – coming to me. Moment-by-moment is like a chain of events, like a pearls of existence put together like a story.

Q: But nobody knows what the next picture would be...

K: The next picture would be the next picture. You don't have to know what it would be. The next would be the next – that you know.

Q: Is there no reason?

K: I didn't say there is no reason. I just said it comes anyway – with or without reason. And the next picture doesn't have to make sense as the picture before never needed to make sense. It's an expression of senselessness. The innocence sensing itself in a chain of events – personal or impersonal or anything. All sensations are sensed by That in-no-sense(innocence). Your very nature is the in-no-sense, realizing itself in senses. There's a sensor, sensing what can be sensed – all that is sensed by what-you-are – without any censorship and not censoring what is sensed. The sensor is sensing what can be sensed.

It's the nature of the sensor to censor. Then there's a story of censorship. It wants to make it a special sense. Like Constantine wants to make a special sense of real life, because he has a censorship up here. This cannot be it, so it has to be something better, something more. You make a censorship – comparison. This is not it, there has to be something what is more real – that's called censorship. That's called mind and the nature of mind is always censoring – judging how it is. That's one way of realizing yourself. Does it make you more or less? Or does it matter?

You cannot change it. The so-called creator wants to make a better creation. It's always good intention. There are seven billion Gods and everyone wants to censor and know better how existence has to realize itself. This is only the humans and not counting the elephants or the animal world. They all know better – how it should be. Everyone knows better than existence. And everyone is comparing and everyone thinks this cannot be it. There has to be something more. This cannot be all.

No. This is all there is.

Q [Another visitor]: In this case, the dog that was waiting for an advantage is dead…

K: You mean the dog doesn't want for a dog-ma anymore. The 'ma' is gone, the mother of all concepts is seen as empty.

Q: It might come back…

K: It may come back. But why not? Nothing is for sure. The temporary absence would be changing to a temporary presence again. So what? As it was, it is and it always will be different. For a while you may remain in – whatever. But then you are stupid enough to pick something up. But does it matter? The main question is does it make you more or less as what-you-are in whatever way you realize yourself or experience yourself. Is there any gaining in gaining and losing in losing? Absolutely not!

All the experiences of gaining and birth and death and the intense life – there's still That what-you-are, what-it-is. Neither changed nor unchanged. By all the changes and non-changes, what-you-are is neither – changed or unchanged – always what-you-are. Never more or less or anything.

So, if you know or don't know – so what? Sometimes there's

knowing, sometimes there's not. Sometimes there's understanding and sometimes not. It's changing always in nature, sometimes it's deeper, sometimes it's higher, and sometimes it's really low and pitiful. So what? How does it matter?

Q [Another visitor]: You say – So what. But still something happened…

K: Where?

Q: I could understand but at the same time – So what…

K: Now she's getting there. [Laughter] In eighth century there was a Tao master sitting somewhere. Everyone came to him with questions and what he achieved and his understanding. And he was just sitting there and saying – So what? And then?

And the question is always – does it make you more or less as what-you-are, and then? And then? What do you want to do with it? With all your fucking understanding. What would you do if you could experience 'real' life? What would you do with it? Would you write a book about it or want to sell it or want to tell your friends? Imagine if you get enlightened and no one wants to know – not even you. What would you do with it?

Q[Another visitor]: The words are so attractive. Even when I know that later there is an ocean of suffering…

K: It's now an ocean of suffering, it was an ocean of suffering and it will be an ocean of suffering.

Q: You talked about the so-called experience of enlightenment as *amok* (psychic disturbance) – it's done…

K: I talked about a relative experience of people who end up in a mad house.

Q: But what remains is an ocean of suffering…

K: A mad person remains – a crazy person.

Q: In one case, sure…

K: In all the cases.

Q: Suppose it's a sage sitting on the chair…

K: It's still mad.

Q: For me, no…

K: You make it special and you want to be special.

Q: I want the best for 'me'…

K: You want the best and best would be special.

Q: Sure…

K: Then be it, I have no contract with you. You may suffer in hell forever by being special – I tell you. I don't want to stop you.

Q: I don't want to be special…

K: Of course you want to be special. Now you don't want to be special – that's really special. Then you are the only one who doesn't want to be special. [Laughter] Come on! You want to be different – and that's special.

Q: I want to be free…

K: And that's special. You want to be the only one that's free. Oh God! Constantine the free one. [Laughter] The only freebie ever – I want to be free. For that he should be imprisoned forever.

Q: As I said before, I just repeat the old words, old concepts that I had read about freedom…

K: Why do you still repeat them?

Q: I don't know. For me the most attractive thing here is…

K: As I told her earlier, you are attracted towards That what never needs to be free.

Q: Yes…

K: You are attracted to freedom – That never needs to be free. But because you want to become it, you are not it. Since you want to own it, you cannot get it. You want to have it and you cannot have it – I tell you. There was never anyone who got it. You can 'be' it – that's the easiest – because you 'are' it. But you can never attain it. You will never have it. It will never be yours.

Never ever was there any ownership in freedom. What kind of freedom would it be that could be owned by Constantine? Constantine's freedom. You can have it forever and no one wants it – Constantine's freedom. [Laughter] Maybe you want to sell it afterwards? Maybe you write a book about freedom.

As I say, would this bloody freedom make you more or less? Would you gain anything by freedom? Or with truth? What would you do with truth if you get it?

Q: That's why I asked – Why is it so attractive?

K: Because you just imagine it. Because you imagine it would be better. It's pure imagination. It's like carrots in front of the donkey and the donkey thinks – if I ever get the carrot I would not be hungry anymore. So, you may run after the carrot. Even if you don't run after the carrot, that's another carrot.

The question is, why should you be better off than the Self? Look at the Self. I'm always pointing out to the helplessness of the Self, of reality that has to realize itself – if it likes it or not. But you want to be a special self who wants to stop this realization. Isn't that fantastic? Crazy! As if life can stop living life. What an idea!

You are That what is life and life has to live life – in whatever possible way. Sometimes is not attractive the way you live life. But still you have to live life in that way. What is the problem? You will never be free. How can one become free? There was never anyone who was born. What is there to be free from?

Q [Another visitor]: It's just a belief…

K: So, you get rid of a belief. But who wants to get rid of a belief? If you know it's just a belief why should you get rid of the belief?

Q: The moment the belief is operating, you don't know that…

K: So what? Does it make you less if you don't know?

Q: You believe yourself to be in that situation…

K: So what?

Q: It's quite a powerful idea…

K: And? You are very powerful and no one else can trick you as you can trick yourself. So what? You are being tricked by yourself. What's the problem?

Q: But you only see that, when the belief is not operating…

K: The moment you want to see that there's no problem, you are dependent on seeing that there's no problem. You still have a problem. You still make it a special seeing. There was never any problem for life, for what-you-are. No life has to see that there's no problem. What kind of life would it be that has to see that there's no problem? That's called Johannes life or Constantine's life or Karl's life.

What do you make out That Absolute life that it has to see that there is no problem to see it as an Absolute life? How stupid do you make that life when you make it like a condition that has to see that there's no problem.

Q: As long as the belief is there, it smells like shit…

K: As long [shouting] That's the biggest word everyone says – as long. You will long forever.

Q: Yes…

K: So, long forever. Consciousness will always long for consciousness. What else can it do? The longing will never stop. You think why does it never stop? Think – Why should it stop? Consciousness is already stupid – that it is conscious. And now it wants to be unconscious because being conscious is now not so fine for consciousness anymore. Now it wants to be unconscious – I don't want to be anymore, says consciousness. I'm fed up by being conscious. [Laughter] What a joke!

Q [Another visitor]: What it really boils down to is that – we were playing a game and we forgot that it was a game and we started to take this game seriously, especially started taking the …

K: The puppet. As I said Shiva starts playing and creates the whole universe – the whole puppet house. Then it starts playing with the puppets and one moment he forgets that he's just playing with the puppets. Then he believes himself to be a puppet. He's hypnotized by his own game. He became a player that is different from the play. Then he doesn't want to be a player anymore because at one point he is fed up of playing. Then he wants to find a way out. But as much as he wants to find a way out, he's in the play. That happens! Shit happens!

You thought in the beginning that you can play around a little bit and nothing will happen and you will go home when you are fed up. Now it's too late, now the play goes on. If you are fed-up or not – you have to play, my dear. You are the play! How can you leave the play? You must be joking.

As long – The moment the long is gone, I don't long anymore. And are you out of the play?

Q: As long is made out of – and then…

K: You see – and then, and then, and then. So, you better be the Zen not in the Zen. Be what-you-are, be what-you-cannot-not-be.

Q: Don't be what you appear to be…

K: No. You are even what you appear to be.

Q: The moment you believe you are what you appear to be, you are in shit…

K: [Jokingly crying] As long and if – those are my favorite words says Johannes. You take them to bed and you wake up with them. [Laughter]

[Singing] As long and if and but. As long and if and why?

[A visitor coughs]

That's your future – coffin. [Laughter]

Q [Another visitor]: Can you clarify, 'So what'?

K: How many watts do you need? You need kilowatts. [Laughter] [Joking] As long as I am a plug, I plug in but when I am unplugged, I'm even the unplugged electricity. That's Johannes. As a plug, I need to plug-in because if I don't plug-in, I'm off electricity. And Constantine too, I really want to plug-in to life because I want to have a 'real' experience of life. Right now I feel so unplugged. [Laughter] And you are always looking for the plug – where is my plug?

Some think there's somewhere my soul-mate where I plug-in forever. [Laughter] I will marry the plug right away if I find the right plug. Then electricity comes – We are one together forever – plug-in. It's actually a plague-in – the idea that you have to be plugged-in. I would rather be dead than to miss a joke.

Constantine thinks if I'm enlightened I'm plugged in. Then I feel alive, the *kundalini* rises and the snake is dancing and *chakras* are in-form. Then Constantine is in glory of all the open chakras. [Laughter]

Q: I know I am very arrogant…

K: You are not the only one. Don't become too arrogant by saying I'm too arrogant. No, you are not alone. [Laughter] There is actually a competition running everywhere – a natural competition of arrogance – Who is more born-apart? The next competition is – who is less born-apart? It's a plague.

Everyone is hoping for the ultimate kick and you hope that the ultimate kick, kicks you out. Then you imagine that being enlightened would be the ultimate kick. [Making a rooster sound] Look at me – Now I'm a rooster and once I was a chicken. I woke up from being a chicken, I chickened out.

It's like once I was a sheep and now I'm a lion. Imagine you are a sheep and you grow up with lions and one day you realize that you are a sheep. [Laughter] That could be fearful, I tell you. That's really – something went wrong. You will be food.

You always want to have a happy end. That's the whole problem here and I show that there's an ugly end – an ugly-duckly end. You will remain an ugly duck forever.

June 15, 2012. Evening Talk.
Mallorca, Spain

There is enlightenment – but only for phantoms

Q: Can you help me?

K: That's permanently there – help, help, help. What do you want? If you want to have a lift to the next city, one can help you. For practical things, one can help each other. But help is only in hell. If someone asks – How can I get out of hell? No! If I would know how to get out, do you still think I would be here? [Laughter]

Q [Another visitor]: It's like I losing a paradise because of my bad English…

K: Lost in translation? But we have a translator here, but she's too late too. She's always too late, even the translator is too late. The moment you understand it, it's too late anyway. It's anyway a misunderstanding. You miss it anyway. That's why Buddha said – misses don't make it, only misters. Women never get enlightened. [Laughter] The sentence continued, but the men just cut the sentence. The next sentence was – Men neither. [Laughter] Women don't get, but men neither.

But men made the Buddhist teachings, so they cut it. Buddha said, women will never get enlightened but the Buddhists didn't complete the sentence. Only Johannes will get enlightened when the sun burns more on his forehead. [Laughter] You will be burnt.

Imagine I could help you, that really would be hell. If there is someone sitting somewhere telling you – I can help you. You should run as far away as you can from there because they cannot even help themselves. But they promise that they can help you. That's only the devil that promises that he can help you.

[Mocking] I will bring you out of hell – but for that you have to do this and this and this. And that keeps you in hell – for sure. Because there is someone in hell and someone promising you to get out of hell – confirms that you are in hell. If you ask me, there's no one in hell, there's only hell.

Q [Another visitor]: What kind of persons were Ramana Maharshi and Nisargadatta in this dream?

K: Nice dream objects. They are just like signs in the dream that there is no one in the dream. But in Reality there was never any Ramana or Nisargadatta. They are just pointing out to the so-called functioning of the body but there's no one. You just give a name and label to some functioning, but there was never anyone who was born.

Q: Some teachers talk about the false sense of authorship is lost. What does that mean?

K: It means nothing. There was no doership before and then there is no doership after. There was never any doership. So, how can one lose it? Maybe they lose the idea that they can lose something. That there is something to change or there's something to lose.

Ramana would say – Devotion of devotion, you give the giving. You transcend the transcending, you renounce the renunciation. All of that is just being what-you-are. So, it's not like someone made it.

Q: But does that happen to someone?

K: No. It never happens to anyone. It's an accident.

Q: Accident in the dream?

K: It's not meant to happen. It never happened to anybody, it will never happen to anybody. That what's the nature of everybody: is already the nature of everybody. Nothing has to happen. It's not a happening, it's a non-event. It's like existence stumbles into something – what is not meant to happen. Then there's just a little split-second – of nothing. But there's no consequence in it. It has no consequence; it has no impact for anybody.

So, whoever tells that after this event this all happened – it's all bullshit. There are some rare guys like Nisargadatta or Ranjit Maharaj, they say that nothing ever happened. But there are many others who say – Since this date, since I fell from the bench, there's a now. Now there's a now. So, there are teachers and there are people who come too late.

And I always meet people who have had enough of it. They have had enough that they have to do something. They are just exhausted – leftovers. [Laughter] Is there a right description for all of you? Look at them – exhausted leftovers. They just hang-on – They don't know for what, but they just hang-on. [Laughter] They don't know anymore why they're here or what they're doing or anything. [Laughter] It's a hangover of existence.

Anyone has any questions? [Silence] Now I should even give you the questions that you should ask me? [Laughter]

Q [Another visitor]: That would be easy...

K: That's more easy for you because you get full entertainment. I would bring two chairs next time – The question chair and the answer chair. [Laughter] Now I would give you answer and you have to find the questions. [Laughter]

This is an exercise that you start laughing about yourself non-stop. Because the joke is that the one that wakes up every morning, to not laugh is quite hard. Make it easy for yourself – Just laugh when you pop-up.

Q: I don't like that...

K: What-you-are is laughing anyway when this clown pops up in the morning and his circus starts. That's very funny that you don't laugh.

Q: But it's not funny for the phantom...

K: No one asked the phantom. No one is interested how the phantom feels. No one wants to know, only the other phantoms want to know. The other phantoms want to check out – How are you today?

Q [Another visitor]: I have a question but I can't find the words...

K: What's the question? Then we can put it in words. [Laughter]

Q: To ask you anything is hopeless...

K: Come on! Just for fun!

Q: When you say rest in that what cannot rest, what is that?

K: Be the Absolute joker but not the joke you experience. You're always joking around. And see the joke as a joke. Because you are the Absolute joker and there will always be the joke – 'me' and the joke will never become the joker.

Q: There's a tendency towards loving and kindness...

K: No. There's no tendency towards love and kindness. It's the opposite, you just want to be left alone and if you would not be kind, they would not let you go. They would just come and complain all the time. You'd rather be kind and lovely. Being lovely is control – you know that. It's all control. Like being lovely to kids, you want to control them and give some tools for survival in life. It's all a preparation for war – being lovely and kind to your so-called kids – giving them tools for survival. And giving them tools for survival because you think being lovely and kind is better for survival.

The intention is that you would like to prepare. You'd like to prepare yourself; you'd like to prepare your kids. It's all a preparation – the whole time. Mind is a tool of preparation – permanently. Preparation for possibilities that you imagine could happen – insurance.

And you want to be sure – about truth, about freedom, about life. You want to be sure because you're afraid. Fear is permanently running your life. All your actions come from fear. You're only kind and lovely because you fear that if you are not, you get beaten up. It doesn't come out of heart, it comes out of fear. The entire bullshit of love and kindness. There are no lovely people. [Laughter] They are just cheaters. The social interaction is just a control mechanism – out of fear – permanently. Relationship – fear, then you try to control the other by being kind and lovely. The man tries to fuck very good so that the wife doesn't go to another man – control.

There is no heaven in this hell – in this bloody life. But that's the beauty. When there really would be kind and lovely people, there would be the other side too. There would be evil people. If you make the one, you get the other side too. But if there are no lovely ones, there are no bad ones. It's good that there are no good ones. There are neither good nor bad ones. It's just a dance of life. And life doesn't need to be lovely or kind to itself. It can be – whatever. It doesn't mind.

The Self cannot be harmed by the Self, existence cannot harm itself – by anything. It cannot kill itself nor can it be born. The rest is – bull-shitting yourself - a bad dream, a nightmare, because every moment you exist, it' a nightmare – moment-by-moment. And you want to get out of that nightmare.

And that's everywhere. You cannot find anyone who's not trying to get out of this nightmare of existence. Show me one and I would shut up forever. Show me one happy person, one kind person, one lovely person and I would not say a word again. You may try now. You may look all over the world and all the universes but you wouldn't find one. All businessmen – run by fear. This relative existence of relative beings is run by fear and driven by insurance companies.

Q: It seems very sophisticated...

K: Very defined and very covered. You put it in the mask of loveliness and kindness. It's just a beast covering it's nature, because you're surrounded by beasts. You are a beast – beastie boys and beastie girls. [Laughter]

Q: Ah well! [Laughter]

K: If you say it as it is, people start laughing. You recognize yourself in it because you have to say – Yes it is like that. If you are really honest you would say – Yes, I am the beast! I am so in love with my fucking self that I would do everything – killing – if just there would be no consequence from it. I would do the worst – just to satisfy myself and you do it anyway. It's all for self-satisfaction.

I'm punching all the phantom beasts because That what-you-are is untouchable in all of that. You can never touch, you can never harm, you can never do anything with it. It is always omnipresent – as what-you-are – which can never be harmed. Nothing can be done to it. It will never change, you cannot alter its nature. Your nature is absolutely uninterrupted – what-it-is. And the rest of the phantom, I will punch to hell.

Q: But the thoughts keep interrupting that...

K: It cannot be interrupted.

Q: Then what is that gets interrupted?

K: It's crap – what can be interrupted.

Q: And there's nothing to do about that?

K: Why should one do anything about crap?

Q: So, I wake into crap?

K: Every morning you wake into the crap – you know that.

Q: The crap wakes up wanting to have a crap... [Laughter]

Q [Another visitor]: Can you see Karl?

K: No. I just close my eyes when I see Karl. It's unbearable to see Karl. That's why I have so much compassion with everyone because everyone has to see Karl. No. If I would sit there, I would kill myself – right away.

Q [Another visitor]: In Mahabharata, Arjuna asked Krishna to show his true form and Krishna said – You wouldn't like it...

K: Yeah. It would kill you right away.

Q: He saw all the lives, the beasts, the death and he asked Krishna to stop...

K: Yeah. You cannot bear it. Nisargadatta said the same – If you really would see the nature of the universe, you would just run for shelter. It's unbearable for anyone. This ocean of pain, this ocean of suffering is unbearable for any relative person. And that's the nature of this – what I call hell. If you really would look into it, you would run away. You could not bear it. No one can bear it because it would kill you.

There are rare guys like Nisargadatta and UG Krishnamurti who point to it. They say – You are not ready for That. No one ever will be ready for That. You will stumble into it when you cannot avoid it. But whatever else you do is trying to avoid That – looking into the true nature of how-it-is. You are not looking for That. You're looking for avoidance, for looking away into nice ideas of truth and freedom and bliss and all of that. You're not looking for That – not by choice. Only when you cannot help it and you have to look, you are made to look for it. But not because you want it.

Otherwise you want to transcend something into the bliss of ecstasy of understanding and truth – all these nice ideas. But not this plain truth which would kill you right away. And it's unbearable for anyone. And rarely people speak about That. They all talk about the blissful space of absence, blah, blah, blah...

But even Buddha said it – There's no way out of this suffering. There is unlimited suffering and unbearable and I'm a total failure because I could not stop it – not even for myself.

Q: Except when they made the four noble truths...

K: But that's the noble truth – You cannot stop suffering.

Q: But that they made it into a practice...

K: You have to practice until a point where no practice would help you. That by no practice, the suffering would stop. And if in that instant of split-second you see the suffering, that there's no way out of that – the idea drops. The idea that there's a way out of it, that's the 'me'. This little hope idea that one day you would get out of That.

But by all the practices, by all the years of practices, Buddha was a total failure and by being a total failure, failing to reach by all means, the idea of a way out drops. And with no idea of a way out, there's no 'me'. There's a peace which was always there. But this little hope of a way out is the 'me'. This little tendency – the tendency of avoidance – that makes the 'me' and the idea that you really can make it.

Bhagavad Gita is the same – Yudhishtara in hell with the question – If this would be for eternity, are there any tendencies left to avoid that? Then by whatever accident, there was no tendency left. He said – May it be forever, who cares? And then – Okay. But not by his choice – never ever. So, nothing can be done for it. But nothing can be done against it too. If it's meant to happen, it will happen. That you cannot avoid this total moment of despair and you cannot close your eyes anymore for That what-is unavoidable. That you are that what is realizing itself and any moment you realize yourself, you realize yourself in separation. You cannot get out of it. That this is discomfort – moment-by-moment. You may call it hell.

Any moment of existence, is an existence of discomfort. But in this way, you realize yourself and it will never stop as it never started. But as a seeker, you always seek a way out. That there would be a moment of – whatever. Then there would be an ecstasy forever and you would be happy ever after... Ha..ha..ha.

Q: The moment my mother died, there seemed to be an incredible energy that came and then it just lifted away like a butterfly on the flower and there was an incredible feeling. What was that?

K: Every time when I was young – butchering a pig, it was the same. It's like a cramp of energy released into the air.

Q: Is that like the bliss?

K: No. It's not like bliss. This little something is entrapped, cramped into a 'me'. Then you cannot hold it anymore and the cramp relaxes and the whole energy opens up.

Q: Isn't it opening up into that…

K: Nothing. It's just opening up into nothing. It doesn't open up in any ocean.

Q: Does it open up into the ocean as you said previously?

K: No. I just said there's an ocean of suffering and you cannot stop it.

Q: So it goes back to the ocean of suffering…

K: No. You don't go into it. There's no 'one' in it, there's just suffering. There's no one going into it.

Q: So, in this suffering there is a freedom from…

K: There's no freedom from anything. You cannot free yourself from the ocean of realization. And you always realize yourself in separation, in the ocean of discomfort. The presence is always discomfort and then in this discomfort, there is more or less discomfort. Then more intense discomfort is being a person and opening up is less discomfortable. But it's still discomfort – more or less discomfort. You can make levels of discomfort.

Q: So, you were sensing it after it was gone, still was it discomfort?

K: Compared to the comfort you are, not even knowing what is comfort, this less discomfort is just a degree of discomfort. But not the comfort, because the comfort can never be experienced. You can only experience yourself in discomfort – levels of discomfort because That what is comfort, the ease itself, can never be experienced. The bliss itself can never be experienced, the peace cannot be experienced. And the rest is just levels and degrees of war – of tension.

Q: Because it's not within our nervous system to experience it?

K: Because there are no two. If there would be an experience of That what is peace, then you would be different from peace. That's impossible. Peace can never be experienced, peace is the absence of two. When there's no two, there's no experience of peace, there's just peace. But never any experience of peace. Whatever you can experience is war, it's tension. And there's intention because wherever there's intention – there's tension – everywhere.

All this is vibration of tension with different intensities and variations of tension. And there's only tension because there is this imaginary two – comparing one with the other. Now you compare the more crampy and the more relaxed. But both are degrees of tension – resistance. Resistance is only there in a dream of two – one resisting the other. More or less resistance, in a dream of whatever-it-is.

And it's never ending. Every night you are very relaxed going to That. Then every morning – shit, again! Temporarily you can say bye, bye – but only temporarily.

Q: In Buddhism they say if you're enlightened, you're supposed to get out of the wheel of incarnation...

K: That's John Wheeler? [Laughter] If even Dalai Lama can't stop the wheel of incarnation – Come on!

Q: In Buddhism they say, if you practice up in the hierarchy, then you are free from the wheel of *karma*. But that's a story anyway...

K: Good luck!

Q: No. I'm not going there...

K: But you still remember very well.

Q: From before...

K: Have more coffee. [Laughter] That's why I try to make it such that you cannot look away from it. It will never be better – never, never. No one ever made it, no one will ever make it because there was no one before who made it and you will not be the first one who will make it. There was no Buddha – Buddha said that. Buddha never showed up. Now you want to do what even Buddha could not do. Who do you think you are? Angelina Jolie wants to have a liver transfer.

When it comes to this life, you run for fucking cover. If you have money, you go and buy a liver. When you have no problem you can have an ethical point of view.

Q [Another visitor]: I don't think that's always true...

K: That's always the case. You will try to survive, it's in-built. There's an in-built survival inside – if you like it or not. If you go to a hospital where you have a cancer patient who is told that he will die next week and if a doctor comes next day saying that if we do this and that, you can live half a year longer, they will will go for it, even when they're finished with life. There's just a disease of hope coming back again. Then you do what the doctor tells you – fuck it all. You are stupid trying to survive in this bloody bullshit body. You cannot help it.

People commit suicide by accident. They normally try to jump and there's a guardian angel who puts them back. Then for once the guardian angel is on holiday.

Q: If I could kill myself, I would...

K: Everyone would kill himself in the morning if he had the guts to do that.

Q [Another visitor]: I'm just too tired in the morning... [Laughter]

K: After coffee? But by then you already have different ideas of what to do on this day. Then it's too late. You sit here for suicide, why do you think you're coming here for? You hope that I kill you

– for that you come. If that's not suicide, what is it? You're fed up of Shalaba and you think I can kill Shalaba. But I have no interest in killing Shalaba because she is quite funny. Why should I kill what entertains me?

It's quite entertaining, she believes she's Spanish, that she's born. That's quite funny. But everyone has different kind of entertainment – some Germans here. They gave up nationality but they're still germs.

Q [Another visitor]: Some people don't care about nationality...

K: But then you care that you don't care.

Q: No...

K: But now you did otherwise you would not even mention it. [Laughter] Now you're proud that you don't care about being Spanish or German. You're even more proud – I'm not special.

Q: I was watching a crime program on television where people tried to kill themselves and I really thought I should also...

K: That depends on the combination of circumstances that decide. If totality doesn't want you to kill yourself, you cannot even if you try as much as you like and even when you want to survive, it may just kill you by accident – as if nothing happened.

Q: But now I want to survive as this body...

K: Then maybe you'd die. [Laughter] But I think that's too much to hope. Some try really hard, they always book Ryan air. [Laughter]

It's a good news that you will never be ready.

Q [Another visitor]: When I go in depression, I find joy. Is depression and happiness the same energy?

K: No. There's only depression – degrees of depression.

Q: I like depression...

K: Everyone likes depression because if there's no depression, you cannot exist as a 'me'. The 'me' is only there when there's this depressed one. It needs some pressure, it needs a circumstance. It can only exist under pressure, without pressure there is no 'me'. The 'me' is created by pressure. This is his field of depression. So, it takes care that he should be depressed.

Then there are degrees of depression because in that you can survive as a 'me' because without a pressure there is no 'me' that can survive. In fact you even fear that there are moments of no depression. [Mocking] Oh! I have to find something, I have to create problems. I like depression – it's a deep-rest.

Q: It's relaxing…

K: For me it's good because then I don't have to work. [Laughter] You can watch television and stay on bed. It's like having a cold. When you're young you need to have a cold and runny nose so that your mother doesn't send you to school but when you've grown up you need to have a reason to stay on bed. You can say – Oh, I'm so depressed today, I'd just watch television. In Spain that's called *siesta*. [Laughter]

Q: If you don't work, you don't get paid…

K: If I don't come, I don't get anything either. We are in the same boat. [Laughter] Problems everywhere!

Q: No hope anywhere… [Laughter]

Q [Another visitor]: Will this depression last forever?

K: Absolutely. You come out of your mother in pressure, then there's depression. Any moment you exist, is depression. You always try to find your precious. You're always under pressure to find yourself. You seek happiness – moment-by-moment. You look for comfort. But you cannot find it because the relaxation you're looking for, you cannot find.

Q: But you would also prefer a relaxed back or neck…

K: You have a technique? Of course! When you're hungry you eat.

When you have stiffness, you try to get rid of it. When you have pain, you take a pill. Why not? By not doing it, you think you can control your tendencies of comfort. But I tell you that this tendency of you always wanting to have comfort, you cannot stop.

All your actions, all your tendencies, the entire universe is run by the tendency for comfort, for harmony. Everything wants to be in harmony. But since everyone is fighting for harmony, there's only war for harmony, not for peace. It will never be reached by anyone. There can be a moment of less disharmony and that you may call peace. You already fear that this peace may go again. There is no real harmony.

The moment you think you're happy, you already fear that you'd lose it again. There is never any experience of happiness in time – Hallelujah and praise the Lord, just-in-case.

Q: Even in the thinking world, sometimes there's too much pressure and then it bursts...

K: And then you're dead. [Laughter] Sounds good. It's like a balloon, you blow into it until it bursts. You are a lunatic anyway – balloonatic – then you blow and make a bigger ego, a bigger 'me'. That was the Osho technique – dynamic blowing. [Laughter] Then you go back and back to your former lives, you become a back-packer. You have a rug sack full of experiences from your former lives.

Q: At one point you remembered that you were never born?

K: No. I don't have to remember that. Even when you forget, you have to-be and in remembering you-are. So, even in forgetting no one forgets and in remembering no one remembers.

Q: Once you were really sure that you have never been born...

K: No one can really be sure. I am born infinite times but by the experience of being born, I am not born because what I Am was before and after that – whatever. And in the meanwhile, nothing happened. There are infinite experiences of birth and death. Moment-by-moment, this moment dies and another moment is born.

Q: But once you realized this…

K: There's no once in it.

Q: If you know this you don't need depression…

K: You don't have to know that.

Q: So, you don't have the pressure within then?

K: Still there is pressure. This love-affair with yourself, you cannot stop because you are under pressure with your precious 'me', the precious self. You give attention to something, you are under pressure. Even if you want to feel good within your body – anything – it's always pressure. Why should it stop? That's the way you realize yourself, as a phantom who wants to be in comfort. And you cannot help it because your nature is helplessness.

You cannot control the dream because you are not in the dream. If you would be in the dream, as the almighty you are, maybe you could alter the dream. But as you are not in the dream, how can you change something where you are not in? You have no influence in all of this.

The Absolute dreamer, because it is not in the dream, it cannot control itself, because for that it needs two. There is no 'once you know something', there is no 'once' in anything. You will never know. You are always That what-you-are inspite of the one who knows or doesn't know. Sometimes this phantom knows and sometimes it doesn't know. [Mocking] Then once a phantom knows that he's not a phantom, then there's a phantom that knows he's not a phantom. But who cares if the phantom knows that he's not a phantom? Only other phantoms care – [Joking] Oh I met a phantom who knows that he's not a phantom, says one phantom – a master phantom, a realized phantom. [Laughter] And I am an unrealized phantom and unrealized phantoms run after realized phantoms.

It's like, once upon a time – the fairy tale continues. Even realized phantoms die – I heard or maybe they live for thousands of years in the Himalayas in Lotus up there and here we are in a locust.

Q [Another visitor]: What is this about thousand years? Who knows what happens after a thousand years?

K: One millennium is gone and then comes the second millennium. Now we are in the third millennium.

Q: Who knows that?

K: The calendar. [Laughter]

Q: People don't even know who they are at their birth and they want to know what happened thousands of years ago or you get reincarnated or not. Who wants to know this?

K: You! Only because of you who now claims not wanting to know it. The one who is on top of everyone who says – Who wants to know that and why is everyone so stupid?

Q: But does anybody know anything?

K: Everybody knows everything!

Q: They think they know...

K: No. They know everything! Ask anyone, everyone knows everything – and for sure better than everybody else.

Q: That's the point...

K: No. That's natural. God incarnated in a phantom knows better than the other phantom Gods – naturally. There's always a Hitler who knows best, what's best.

Q: Nobody knows anything...

K: Everybody knows everything. [Laughter] Ask them. Shalaba knows everything and she's a moralistic institution. She's the universal point of ethics. She totally knows ethics. She has an ethic, tic-tac.

Q: Are you saying people suffer everyday?

K: No. People don't suffer, how can they suffer?

Q: They want to know what would happen after thousands years, isn't that stupid?

K: Why not? If even to exist is stupid, then why is that especially stupid? It's all stupid.

Q: We can't even deal with the life now...

K: Who needs to deal with life? Life deals with you, I tell you. [Laughter] I think that's the opposite. It's your number that's being dealt with.

Q: I ask you because I have not read the books about various masters...

K: Maybe you should.

Q: I have not read them because as you said, one just knows that...

K: Who said it? I never said that. Don't put me in that bullshit. You offend me, I'll kill you!

Q: People write books...

K: No! Thank God I never wrote any book.

Q: When we are children, we are taught that this is a table and that is a chair. How can we know it is really like you experience it?

K: How can we know that's a table? But we still call it a table. Then you say I don't know if it's a table but maybe it's a table. I really don't know, but they call it a table.

Q: But that's necessary for the sake of practical conversations...

K: So, what's wrong with that?

Q: That's okay, but when they talk about spirituality, people read books and have spiritual experiences. How can they know if it's that what's written in the book? And who knows that?

K: And who needs to know that they know? You now want to know if they know. You are questioning – Do they really know?

Can they really be sure? Now you want me to work and I'm not here for work. [Laughter] I'm not in the Byron Katie drama. It sounds like Byron Katie – Can you really be sure? Can it really be true? How can you know that? What would you be without it? [Laughter] It is as it-is.

Q: You say that you were never born and you would never die...

K: No. I say what-you-are was never born and will never die. But that what speaks now is born and it will die. So, that what speaks now is already dead. You are That – Dead! [Laughter]

Q: How do you know That what-you-are was never born and will never die?

K: That what I Am doesn't need to know That and That what is pronouncing That he's not born, for sure is born. What-you-are doesn't need to say – I am not born and that what says – I am not born, for sure is born.

Q: How do you know?

K: I just said whoever said what-you-are is never born is already born and is bullshit. What is – That what-it-is, never needs to say what-it-is. Even to say I Am unborn is a bloody concept. How often do I have to say that whatever can be pronounced is bullshit? If you say – I am born, that's bullshit. If you say – I am unborn, that's the same bullshit. Whatever starts with 'I' is bullshit. You can say – I Am Shit.

Q: That's what I say, there's no hope...

K: No hope is still too much hope. You define it and now you say – Now there's no hope as if there was hope earlier.

Q: There's a point where you know that happiness is just temporary...

K: And unhappiness too.

Q: So I am here for what?

K: I don't know why you are here for. Maybe to pay some money. [Laughter] You are here so that I can pay my bills – just practical. If you start asking why am I here for, then you're really in shit. When you question all the masters, then you are the biggest master. Then you think you know more than everyone else. Then you are really special and in the special hell and I don't mind that you're in that special hell.

I have no interest in getting anyone out of their self-made hell – self-employed in his own hell. You are the master and the slave in the same moment – in the slavery of your bloody concepts of mind-fucking – being the fucker, fucking the fucker. Do you think I have any interest to stop that? Why should I care? I don't want to change a thing. You can be the biggest asshole on earth, a murderer, a killer and you would still be what is that – what is me. And there's no spot on you and you have never done anything in your nature. And the rest doesn't count anyway.

So, who cares about the one who knows or doesn't know? What-you-are is knowledge itself and never needs to know anything and would never say I am born or unborn. And that what says I am born or unborn are fucking, cheating masters.

Q: Whatever you said, I could have never thought of these things...

K: Then why do you now?

Q: Because I am here...

K: Just get ear plugs and listen to backstreet boys. [Laughter]

Q: Someone put me on this horse...

K: And now you are stupid enough to ride.

Q: I want everything to be as it was before...

K: For that you will have to be re-born, now it's too late. [Laughter] The chair doesn't want to be a chair but still has to be a chair. And the chair cannot decide which asshole sits on it. [Laughter] That's your position – now it's too late. Existence is like a chair that takes every asshole on.

Q [Another visitor]: I have another concept – nothing-is...

K: That's too much. Many say that – nothing is real. That's bullshit because no-thing is still a thing, no-time is still time. Who defines what-is and what-is-not? It's all too late. The moment you open your bloody mouth, it's too late – shit happens. Relative words of relative bullshit. Even nothing-is, is relative bullshit. Imagine, if only nothing would be! You would be bored to death.

Q: It's an eloquent concept, I bought that for a while...

K: One is stupid enough to buy everything. To go to church and listen to the preacher. You listen to yourself in the morning – that's worse. You start thinking and start talking to yourself. Nothing is worse than that. You wake up and ask – How am I today? How did I sleep? What shall we do today? What do we have to do? Making plans – as if you can make plans.

Q: Your jokes are too fast for me...

K: For me too, I can't even laugh between the jokes – what a pity. I should laugh and enjoy, but even before that comes another joke.

Q [Another visitor]: I don't like the thoughts that come...

K: Welcome, well-go. What to do? They come as uninvited guests and stay for whatever time and they go automatically. They come automatically and go automatically. What to do with them?

Q: Who wants them to go?

K: Another thought. There's a guest that doesn't want to share the space. Then it fights other guest thoughts – I want to be alone – fuck off, leave me alone. It's like a host-ghost. the host doesn't want to have a guest. It's a guest house but it's closed for today. Then an uninvited guest comes and the host thought says – We are closed now! You have to wait until we open again, I'm meditating now. Come later when you have an appointment. You're not on my calendar – piss-off. Then you fight and are involved in that.

Q: So, it's the same phantom always there?

K: The phantom wants to rule and decide when the next thought would come and go. It wants to be a ruler because it fears that the uninvited guest would kick him out. He wants to be stabilized in a single thought. So, he permanently defines how he is – I am like this and not like that. That's my father and that's my mother, always knitting the story – past, present, future. Without that there's no 'me'. So, it's always involved knitting it's own story, spinning its network of 'my friends', 'my enemies', what I have done or not done – the entire story.

Then I sit here and tell you – It's his-story – the phantom's story and you have no influence in it. What can you do with it? Just see that the phantom has a story and you cannot help it. You have to be what-you-are inspite of the presence and the absence of the phantom and how the story is. The phantom will always spin a story.

It's like a spider whose nature is spinning. What can you do against the nature of a spider? Try to make it not spin? The mind has to think. That's his bloody nature – minding the mind, moment-by-moment. So, what's the problem with it? Only when you create a second mind, a second opinion. Then you compare which one is a better mind. Then mind says, I would be a better mind with no-mind – says the mind. Then it says nothing would be better than something. I would be better-off if I would be nobody... blah, blah, blah. Always making concepts because without making concepts, it cannot survive as the first concept. It always needs to be surrounded by concepts of past, present and future, blah, blah, blah.

Then there are others, other masters and other people. Then defining how they are and the bullshit that they say. Why do they do that? Blah, blah, blah. Why? Why? Why? Always why? Why is he enlightened and not me? Why he woke up and not me? I was much more interested and I would fit much better in that chair. [Laughter] Some already buy a dress and imagine how it would be to sit there and get all the attention from everybody. They are all posters in front of the mirror every morning. [Laughter] There are even training camps – preparation for advaita teachers.

Q [Another visitor]: Yeah, he even does it online! [Laughter]

K: Non-duality camps! In Moscow there are many enlightened ones. Every day a new one pops-up. [Laughter] It's all a theater. It's all a big circus of bullshit. But what to do? You cannot get rid of it, because it's your bloody circus. Complaining – it's fun, but does it help? No.

Q: So, even the phantom is a thought?

K: It's just a popping up thought with all the surrounding thoughts. It's like a sun surrounded with planets of secondary thoughts. It's like the main thought 'I', then it gathers a universe of other thoughts. That's called the cluster – 'me'. A cluster of concepts which are the functioning of a 'me', of a personality. It's just like a cluster of concepts. And when this body dies, this cluster just disappears and the person was never there. It was just a cluster of ideas.

Q: So, there is no phantom?

K: A cluster of ideas is the phantom – of a personal story – that's all. Just an energetic cluster of memory effects, of stories – past, present and future stories. The whole blah, blah, blah – 'me' – coming from another cluster of blah, blah, blah. Cluster creating clusters.

So, when I talk to you, should I talk to the cluster or That what is the nature of the cluster? That's the question. If I talk to the nature, there's no problem. If I talk to the cluster, for sure there are tendencies for making it a nicer cluster. And the cluster always wants to be the best cluster – very defined with a defense system running so that you are always safe and sure. All your concepts are very defined and stable and you can really stand up for your ethic moralistic things. Shalaba is an example for that. I rarely meet people that have such a high standard of ethic and moralistic point of view.

And you cannot help it. In the morning the 'I' pops up and it gathers all the soldiers around it – like a general with all the little soldiers. Sometimes there's a democratic election – Who is the general today? And then the little fight starts already – It's 'me', we have to do this and this, we should go to war. Then the other one says, but I am a peace maker, maybe that would be better. Maybe we should talk to the tax person politely and then we have to pay less. It's like being in a chicken store where everyone wants to be a rooster but they are all chicken. Then one chicken plays a rooster. [Laughter]

You will always talk to yourself – if you like it or not. You cannot stop talking to yourself. You realize yourself by talking to yourself and explaining what-you-are. You have to explain the door that there can be a door, you have to explain the universe that there can be a universe. You have to give it a name otherwise you cannot experience it. This is the way of realizing yourself in all the different ways. How else can you experience your finger if you don't call it a finger?

You can only realize yourself in differences. By not giving it a name, there's no finger, you don't even see it. Like a baby that doesn't see any world. Then slowly by words, it starts seeing the world more and more. It puts a pattern of a world together – like a puzzle. Without naming something, it's not there. It's amazing.

Q [Another visitor]: But our perception is made like that...

K: But what's the problem with it? Do you want to have everything at once all the time? Greedy bastards! [Mocking] No, I don't just want to see the little finger, I want to see the hand. They now make glasses where you can only see one point at a time, the rest you have to imagine. No one gets a holistic view, only a tunnel view. And the rest is just at a periphery somewhere – you have to fit it together. You can only see through this little narrow 'thing'. Crazy! The rest is there but it's an imagination. You're not sure what's there anyway.

But what's the problem with it? Does it make you more when you have a bigger view? Or less when you have a smaller view?

Q: The Absolute dreamer is realizing itself in little…

K: In little bits? Does Reality gets more real through a bigger view? Or less when its very knitty-knitty?

Q [Another visitor]: No…

K: So, what's the problem? But 'me' – I want to have a bigger view.

Q [Another visitor]: I met a teacher that talked about the annihilation of the phantom…

K: Those are the worse guys. At least I tell you that whatever I say is a lie. [Laughter]

Q [Another visitor]: But it's his truth…

K: That's the problem. That he has a truth. And the truth you can have, what kind of truth would that be? The truth that can be owned and can be reached, that can be named and framed – what kind of truth would that be? And then sold as 'Brilliant Stillness'

Q: But it is the 'presence' – what-it-is…

K: If it would be the presence, it would not be the absence. That's his landing place. Everyone lands in the presence – in the 'Perfect Stillness' of presence. Then everyone else is jealous about him. They say – You could be there too. Fuck it all!

Q: He says he's not there…

K: But 'he' claims that he's not there. Then they're really clever. They say – I am the presence. It's tricky, it's a very big trap because you want to be there too and there's one who promises something.

Q: He's not promising…

K: But it's a promising state.

Q: Yeah.

K: Of course he's promising – that he made it. And if can make it, you can make it too.

Q: He doesn't say he made it...

K: But he says he stumbled into, like an accident. Ha..ha..ha... [Laughter] Even bloody UG Krishnamurti wrote about it in his book the Mystique of Enlightenment. He said that I stumbled into the total mystery without any intention. But then later he said – The bullshit of enlightenment. He even destroyed the first book he wrote and all that mystery.

Q: So, is there nothing called enlightenment?

K: There is enlightenment – but only for phantoms. There is, but there is-not. You cannot say there is not because then you claim that you know better than existence. There is, but there is-not. In dream – yes, but in reality – there was never one and never will be one who was enlightened. But in the dream there are many enlightened and unenlightened ones. But – in the dream.

So, yes there are but there are not. Who needs to be still and brilliant and unique and perfect? Perfect Brilliant Stillness. [Laughter] How can there be brilliant fucking stillness?

Q [Another visitor]: But this stillness swallowed you in seventies?

K: Nothing swallowed me. For years I sat in Tiruvannamalai and said – What I Am is prior and beyond. If you ask me now – What a bullshit! That's why I sit here – You ask me about the experiences I had and I say that's all bullshit. It's all a fairytale of existence. All the experiences of being sucked into a black hole of whatever kind – is bullshit. It's all a story of a phantom Karl. So what? Nothing happened.

What's the problem if I have a nice coffee in this shop or that shop? Or having a spiritual experience? What's the difference? It's all a bloody sensational experience of a bloody Karl. It's all a story of a blah, blah, blah – cluster of an energetic Karl.

And if even the entire existence gives me a blow job as Karl, it will be a very nice experience. But it will be a story. What a blow job! But it was a suck job. But if everything is anyway a trap, why destroy it? If I now say that I have to remove my story from my homepage, now I have to cleanup everything, then I would give it importance. Then I would make it special. Then I would make it really important as if now I know better.

I know as much bullshit now as I knew then. I am absolutely lazy. I don't care what people think about it or not. I really give a shit if people think I am realized or not or know anything. That's why people come because I really give a shit if they believe me or not. I have nothing to gain here if anyone believes in whatever I say or not. It's like stay or leave or fuck-off, it would not make me more or less as I Am.

That's what you come for. For the carelessness and not that you care that in the seventies I dissolved into the black hole, blah, blah, blah. Who gives a fuck about it if there was a vacuum?

This carelessness – that's the most attractive thing. If there was something or there was nothing – Who gives a bloody fuck about if that's true or not? People come to me and say, you said this thirty years ago. It's like people asking Nisargadatta about questions on I Am That. If you asked him later about I Am That, he said – What a bullshit! You can just burn the entire book. But even to say that is too much.

Q [Another visitor]: I have become lazier. I have lost enthusiasm to do things as before…

K: Sounds good.

Q: I feel guilty about not doing things…

K: Then you are not lazy, then you just resist. But who gives a shit about what you said a minute ago? All the promises you gave to yourself. Now you define yourself as lazy – that's too much work. You better be really lazy because you are too lazy to be lazy. Right now you are working too much on your laziness. I am too lazy to be lazy because it's hard work to be lazy.

Look at Prakash, he is always exhausted by being lazy. [Laughter] If you especially not want to do something – Today I don't do anything.

Q [Another visitor]: Who are you?

K: I only have these meetings that someday someone will come and tell me who I am. That's a permanent question.

Q [Another visitor]: Do you have a phantom?

K: Everyday another one. Every day a new one pops up, slightly different one. It's never the same, every moment is different. If you really look for it, you cannot find the same phantom that was five minutes before. It's always different – always slightly different. You really have to remember – How was I yesterday? I don't want to shock people by not being stable. Maybe they would put me in a mad house if I'm everyday different.

But you are always a different mixture of cocktail of tendencies, memory effects of what comes and goes. You cannot even control what memories come because out of those memories, there's a construction of a 'me'. You cannot control what pops up from which side and which dream you get and who was sucked in late seventies in the black hole? Who was it? The left Karl or the right Karl or the upper Karl or the lower Karl? The sucked Karl or the sucker Karl? Aren't we all a bit sucker and sucked?

You always have to make this decision – Am I the fucker or the fucked? [Laughter]

Q: We are always the fucked...

K: No. Sometimes you believe that you're the fucker and sometimes you're the fucked and sometimes and you're neither. Then you're really in trouble. Then you have to find your place again – Am I the fucked or the fucker? What the fuck am I doing here?

Q: How old are you?

K: You don't want to know. Even I don't want to know. [Laughter] I can even speak about the fifties. But now I can say that – I am not even born. [Laughter]

*October 4, 2012. Evening Talk.
Mallorca, Spain*

Consciousness wants nothing from you, it's just having fun

Q: I had many dreams at night but I don't remember them now. Maybe your eyes are too strong...

K: People tell me that but I have no idea. When I shave, I rarely look at my eyes.

Q [Another visitor]: We even forget what you say...

K: No. You never got it. How can you forget it?

Q: Yesterday Johannes asked – What is the final liberation?

K: What is non-final?

Q: Don't ask me... [Laughter] But he could not remember what he said nor do I...

K: Not even me. [Laughter]

Q [Another visitor]: You said kill yourself...

K: That's the most famous answer for this question – Kill your self, kill the idea that there's a self. Then there's no one who needs to be liberated – that's final. Very simple.

Q [Another visitor]: But that never happens...

K: It happens every night, every night you kill yourself – the idea that there's a self and just be in the absence. It's very natural – every night you kill your bloody self. You forget yourself, otherwise you cannot sleep.

Q: I mean in the awakened state...

K: Who can do that? You cannot do it because if you could do that, the doer remains. That's not killing. That's just temporary – fucking yourself without a fucker. Everyone is an expert at killing oneself every night. Prakash took six hours and could not kill himself last night. That's why he looks today like this. [Laughter]

Q: Me neither. I tried to sleep and I had nightmares...

K: Every dream is a nightmare. Like this is a nightmare.

Q: But at least at night you take the nightmare away for a while...

K: No. It just waits around the corner. The moment you wake up, it's back. You just turn away for it and then it waits for you.

Q: What I mean is there maybe a little time of deep-deep sleep...

K: Without that you could not survive, the body cannot take it for long. That's why people die, they get exhausted after sixty, seventy, eighty years. They get exhausted by trying to kill themselves.

Q [Another visitor]: Which one is more important, the deep-deep sleep phase or the dream phase?

K: That you have to watch now. [Laughter] I give you an hour to watch your deep-deep sleep and then you can compare it with your dream state. The deep-deep sleep is uncomparable. Why do you compare?

Q: Because I'm stupid...

K: But you don't have to remind us all the time. [Laughter] Many talked about that, in deep-deep sleep there's no one to complain. Nothing is better than that. When he asked me what is final liberation? That is when there's no one to be liberated – never was, never will be. As there was never any one who needed to be liberated. Who cares if the phantom is liberated? Only the other phantoms.

Moksha is the absolute absence of a necessity of liberation.

Q [Another visitor]: Does That happen to someone?

K: No, never happened to anyone. No one needs to be jealous because it never happened to anyone. No one ever reached liberation. No one ever became himself. Imagine! Does your Self become you? No, because when Self is, you are not.

Q [Another visitor]: I dreamt of a big tsunami wave that kills me...

K: Every night. A tsunami – the 'me' drops. The darkness swallows the light and only darkness remains. Then in the morning, the absence spits out the light – the first light of awareness. Then this bullshit starts again and the darkness doesn't mind. It is still the darkness – with and without the light. So, where's the problem?

Know yourself as you know yourself in deep-deep sleep – just be That – what is the darkness. That darkness is the Reality realizing itself in light. That's all I'm talking about. And the darkness has no interest to stop it because it's never harmed by it or has any discomfort. How can the Absolute be in discomfort? Discomfort can only be in the idea of two – when there's one in something.

You got it now – go home. [Laughter]

Q [Another visitor]: I'm wondering why am I still coming here?

K: As she said, you keep getting stupid again. That's the main tendency. By waking up, the darkness falls in love with the light. Then the love affair continues – becomes a lover and creates all the concepts of liberation, of God – out of the love for the self. Fuck it all!

And you cannot help it. I'm just telling you – there's no guilt in that. There's no sin because you cannot not fall in love. It's just a very natural tendency of waking up and then falling in love with the first light. Love at first sight – and then it's already too late. Whatever you do to stop that, makes it continue. Trying not to love yourself, is out of love. Everything is out of love. What to do?

You are not the only stupid one, even the masters are stupid. Look at me, I'm still sitting here. Stupid enough to talk to you, but helplessness seems to be the nature because you cannot help yourself. You are the knowledge itself but in your realization you are as stupid as you can be. Love makes you so fucking stupid.

Sometimes it's not so nice – this passion. You suffer for your beloved. For who else would you suffer? Only for your beloved self, you suffer and suffer – out of love.

Q [Another visitor]: What does 'your beloved self' mean? Is it the phantom?

K: No. It's your self. You want to become your Self so your beloved Self is your nature. But trying to become what is your nature, you suffer by not being your nature. You make your beloved self – your higher self, your very self – your inner self. And then you love it so much. Then you are full of passion to reach it. But as much as you want to reach it, you miss it.

Missing your beloved self – is misery. Missing your beloved happiness, your beloved knowledge, your beloved truth, freedom – all that you are in nature. You fall in love with what-you-are and then you miss it. Then you run after it and seek it. Then you are sick. No one is as sick as the self that is looking for the self. The seeker who's seeking the seeker. What a stupid thing!

There is no beloved outside. You only love yourself – you know that already. You never loved anyone besides yourself. Or not?

Q: Yeah...

K: You look for someone who has more money or a better body. You are not loving any outside object, you are only in love with yourself. You're only in love with comfort, with happiness, with freedom. These are your tools. You go out with a man or a woman or masters because you want to use them as tools to reach your self. Just abusing everything. You are the biggest abuser of all time. [Laughing] Then you rape yourself and then it hurts. It's crazy!

Only love can make you do that, being so ruthless to yourself. To your inner and outer self because this love brings you so much pain and pleasure and it's so unbearable – this relative love with yourself – that you would kill everyone for that, if there would be no consequences.

You go to war, you shoot people. For nothing else you would do everything – only for your beloved self, you would do everything. And that beloved self has so many names – truth, God, freedom. Everyone gives a different name but it's always beloved with different name. You even have children for that because then you think you will love something more than yourself. But it doesn't work.

Q [Another visitor]: It works...

K: No it doesn't. Some mothers kill them if the limit is crossed.

Q: Normally even when they kill you, you don't complain...

K: Normally you are happy when they are out of the home because they found out that the children could not give the happiness that they are looking for. They are just doing their duty because the conditioning of the surrounding makes them do that – like mother Mary. She realized her Self by seeing her son die. Then the love of a mother was broken and she saw no hope and could not bear it. Then a limit was crossed and she became the black Madonna. Then she was realized as that which was never born and never had any son, but there are always limits and degrees where this can happen.

So, even the love of the mother would break – sooner or later. It has to break. It's just a technique of consciousness to create circumstances of imaginary heart breaks, the imaginary love affair with someone else. The Bible says – You shouldn't love anyone more than your self. And if you do, you would suffer.

Q: My daughter broke my heart I you still love her...

K: No. Then she didn't really break your heart. You are just disappointed, you still hope and that's not a broken heart. Maria was lucky because her son died. There was no possibility of a hope anymore.

Q: That's the worst thing that can happen to a mother...

K: No. That's the best thing for a mother.

Q: I see many mothers lose their children...

K: Then they turn inwards, they turn away from the world. That's what consciousness wants to do. But it's not so bad. What's wrong with it? Consciousness creates all the circumstances, so that the self turns away from the world. If that doesn't happen, if it's not strong enough, you cannot blame consciousness. It tries very hard to get rid of the idea that the world can make you happy. If it doesn't work, that's not the fault of consciousness. It's just your resistance.

Q: In my case, I would still like to think that's not the case with my daughter. I don't trust consciousness in that way...

K: You cannot trust consciousness in anyway. If something has to happen in future, it will happen anyway, if not, not. If I talk about it or not it doesn't matter. If it has to happen, it will happen anyway. If that's needed for consciousness in your case to turn away from the world, it will happen.

Q: Don't say that... [Laughter]

K: I would say it.

Q: I would give up this seeking right now...

K: I tell you, it's all unpredictable. The darkest thing that you cannot expect, if that has to happen, it will happen. You will die – that's the worse thing that will happen anyway. The worst scenario is already certain. The mother will die – you will be gone. If you die now or twenty years later – who cares?

Q: But for mother, the worst case scenario is to lose a child...

K: That was mother Mary. That was the best for her. That's the symbol that the heart of the mother has to be broken for That. If you still want to hold on to that and want to have a preference, that makes you suffer. Even the idea that it may happen, makes you suffer already. That's the nature of suffering – holding on to an idea – being a mother, that's the worst idea.

Q: If I could go back, I wouldn't have my daughter...

K: You're already regretting. It's like me, I regret that I fucked first. If Ramana would have been twenty when it happened and he had fucked girls before, he would have been a house holder for the rest of his life and not sit on a mountain. You never know. But since he didn't have sex, the whole thing was gone for him. Now they say you have to be a celibate. But I tell you if Ramana had a good sex life before, he would just have continued – like eating. How does it make a difference, having kids or not?

It's just a fear of getting hurt and everyone wants to avoid getting hurt. It doesn't even have to break your heart – and that breaks your heart. You can continue to be a bloody mother or anything. It really breaks your heart, that there's no one who needs to break your heart. That's really breaking of the heart. That nothing has to happen, in anyway. And nothing will happen anyway. Bloody heart. Keep your heart forever – no one cares.

Existence absolutely doesn't care if you have a heart or not and if you suffer or not. The carelessness of what-is is absolute careless about all your feelings and your heart. Everyone thinks existence takes care of them, consciousness wants something from you. Consciousness wants nothing from you, it's just having fun. Consciousness is not interested if you get liberated or not or has any idea of understanding or any final liberation or anything. It really gives a shit about what happens to you – all the time. And you know that, as you give a shit about anything – all the time. Selfish! [Laughing]

That's the good news – you are free already. No one wants

something from you. You don't have to be special, you don't have to be understanding. It doesn't have to be some kind of – 'I am more aware' bullshit. Or 'I'm now the witness and consciousness' [claps] – Bravo! You made it! Now I embrace you! Bullshit! As if consciousness embraces you and you get a gold medal on your shirt as an Olympic winner of all time awareness game. [Laughter]

Isn't it fun? Just for sport. This big tiger plays with you like a little mouse and it's not even hungry. It just plays around with you. This idea that there's grace that takes care of you – awfully bullshit bah, bah, bah. [Mocking] A *baba* that takes care.

Q [Another visitor]: But everything is grace...

K: No. Grace is bullshit. [Laughter] You can say your nature is grace. But grace doesn't need grace. There's no grace for what-you-are. There's no self for what-you-are. There's no God, there's no bliss, there's nothing what you talk about. It's all imaginary bullshit from an imaginary phantom, having an imaginary truth or imaginary grace – out of fear.

It's really amazing. All for fun. Unbelievable! All my precious insights, all my precious things and all what I have done and suffered – all for nothing. [Mocking] Does it really have to be for nothing? I went through all those nights of not sleeping and fucking with my mind about who I am. All for nothing!

Q [Another visitor]: I was really angry when I realized it was all for nothing. Twenty years of fighting for nothing...

K: There are two possibilities after that. You start laughing for ever after that or you get depressed and angry but you cannot decide. Half of them get angry and depressed and really want to kill everybody including oneself. Even the Self they want to kill. Or they keep laughing and laughing, saying – What a joke! Sometimes you start being depressed and after a while you see joke in that and then the laughter remains.

Q [Another visitor]: For m e it's amazing, that people understand each other at all...

K: For me, that's natural because consciousness doesn't need to listen to understand. Before someone says something, That what-you-are knows what he would say – instantly. Because infinite times you have already heard it and you are That what is speaking and listening. You know it by nature, you don't even have to listen. That happens with people sometimes, they don't listen anymore but they understand. They cannot memorize and if you ask them later they'd say maybe I have not understood anything. But That what is there – just understands by being what-it-is. It doesn't even need to listen to what is being said.

Q [Another visitor]: Is that true in your case?

K: When I look into your eyes, I know what's going to come – Shalaba comes. [Laughter] It's amazing because many people say that you answer before I ask. I have to always keep quiet and allow the question to happen. It always wants to come out even before you open your mouth. Strange. And then they say – you are impatient. No, I'm not. I'm more than impatient. I could kill you right away. [Laughter]

Q [Another visitor]: That's true because before coming here this morning, I was thinking about dreams and you already started talking about dreams before we even spoke…

K: It happens. Consciousness plays all the roles and knows exactly what happens.

Q [Another visitor]: I would like to ask about intuition…

K: That's consciousness – knowing everything already. Very simple. You know if your mother-in-law calls you or not. Someone calls you on phone and you already know who it is before even you pick it up. Now you even have a name on the phone, so you know it naturally. [Laughter]

Q: Can I choose to trust it?

K: No. You cannot trust anything. Sometimes your intuition says the opposite of what happens. You have a really good feeling about the next boyfriend, but the next morning, he's gone. Sometimes you don't even meet him but you have the intuition that today he may come. [Laughter] I feel very strongly that the next boyfriend will appear. Then the day goes by and nothing happens. Many people go to astrologers and then say – Today is the day. Then they're looking around. They should look into the mirror and the boyfriend is already there. [Laughter]

Q: In my view, it is really triggered by the thoughts that are in your mind...

K: You never know. Maybe it's triggered by the thought of a future which is already there. You never know what's making that thought happen. Maybe, you have to think how the future should be – as the future already is. So, the future creates the thoughts now. Then you can say – Oh, I already thought about it, because you have to say this in future, and you will say it, thought would happen now. It's all inter-related.

The future is already there and the future demands that you now have the experiences so that the future can be as the future already is.

Q: Then I think that was intuition...

K: Yeah. That you can say it was intuition, now you have to have that intuition.

Q: If I have two places to chose from, I feel strongly about one place where I have to go...

K: Yeah because you have to be there, so you have to go there.

Q: But how does that work?

K: It works because the future makes the decision now so that in future you could be where the decision now leads you. You cannot divide it. Both are inter-related. Actually it's the total circumstance that dictates what happens and not your intuition. You never decided anything. Decisions are made by the future.

That we are now sitting here and the past had to happen exactly the way it did, so that this can happen. And whatever will happen in future demands that from now on you do this, so that the future could be as the future already is. And there's no way of changing it.

Q: Can I see the source of the thinking process?

K: Whatever you have done leads to what is now. And whatever will happen in future will happen, so that the future is like it should be. It's not anyone's decision – never was. It's already fixed. Every word I say – is already spoken.

Q: By whom?

K: It doesn't need anyone. Every event has already happened. So, by all the future events nothing happens because the future events have already happened. Everything in this moment is a potential of all the future moments. This is an absolute potential of everything – future, past, everything you can imagine is here-now. It's all fixed, nothing can be changed anymore because everything already has a blue-print, here-now.

[Clapping] This is the beginning and end of everything. [Making sounds of beaming light] Shrrp... Shrrp...

That's peace. I'm talking about peace – silence. Nothing can happen anymore because everything happened already. So, why do you fear? Even the fear you cannot avoid because even the fear is necessary. If you cannot get rid of the fear or anything, what to do?

Just be what-you-cannot-not-be, the next sip of coffee, the next thought. The next is unavoidable – So what? It's simply the next realization of what-you-are which is absolutely fixed. Even you as the almighty self cannot change the destiny of the next moment. Whatever you experience is – destiny, destiny, destiny. And no one made any choice for that. No one could ever change it.

So, the Absolute reality cannot change the next moment of realization.

Q [Another visitor]: Some people say – You can plan. So, can I choose it?

K: People say just the opposite. You can trust the people or listen to what I say. People need the hope that they can do something. Without the idea that you can do something for the future to change, to control, there's no 'me'. Where's the 'me' without the idea that you can do something? And that by your doing the future would change? Without that idea, there's no doership, there's no 'me'. How can that happen?

Phantom is the phantom idea that you by your doing, alter the future, that you can change life. That's the idea of a 'me' inside and that little arrogant one inside is always pissed because what he wants, doesn't happen. That's like a little arrogant God who could not change his own destiny. He's so pissed and fucked and aggressive and hates everything. He wants to destroy the whole life – If I cannot get what I want, I don't want the whole universe to be and everyone is like that. When you are on the street, you are God driving his car and then everyone else is a bad driver. Only if everyone would drive like me! Only if everyone would be as honest as me! Or everyone would be 'whatever' as me! Then the world would be – wow!

God in his nature is the biggest fascist – ever. He always wants to change himself because he's never good enough for himself. The beloved is never lovable enough for the lover. He cannot love himself because he's never perfect. Then come these books – Brilliant Stillness tra..la..la.. Then someone sees his beloved as perfect – Ha, ha, ha. A temporary pause – Today my beloved is doing what I want.

It's just a temporary bullshit. It will never hold what is promised. If it really would be true, then why is it not for everyone that way? If it really would be the truth, it should be the truth for everyone. If it's just for one – Perfect Stillness – Who cares? If that really would be a reality, then it should not be different in any case.

But mainly all the Gods are fucked and pissed and disappointed with their own destiny and that's more natural, as I see it. It's natural to be pissed with what happens and disagreeing with oneself. Even if you are the Absolute source of all that bullshit, you will ask yourself – What am I doing? Then you see the babies getting killed and all the nastiness that you can do and it breaks your heart.

But it doesn't break your heart because you have to see that – again and again what comes out of your so-called realization. All this ocean of suffering, billions of beings suffering as they are – no one can take that. Then sometimes seeing this 'Brilliant Stillness' is a temporary understanding. That has to happen too – just as an opposite.

But you have to be what-you-are in the presence of that unlimited suffering, the unlimited passionate affair with yourself which is an unlimited depression and discomfort. And even seeing everything as perfect stillness is a discomfort because there's a need for it. And if you don't see it like that, you suffer again. So, you need to see it as perfect stillness so that you don't suffer.

It's a needy bastard. The moment God sees his creation as good, he depends on being good. No, there's no salvation for anybody – not even for God. And there's no need for it. Who needs to have salvation? Assholes. Only assholes need salvation – so that they can open up. [Laughing] I always come to the point. [Laughter]

I'm talking about the joy that you don't have to enjoy your fucking relationship. There's no need for enjoying anything. You don't need peace – peace-off. You don't have to make peace with yourself – bullshit. All these ideas come out of a devilish idea that there's a second self, that there's really a lover and a beloved and all this dream bullshit that you're continuing to have with yourself. Blah, blah, blah.

It's fun. You read all these books and you get jealous about the 'one' who can see everything as perfect stillness. [Laughter] What a joke! I tell you that everyone who wakes up is in unconditional hate. And this maybe makes the hate for himself bearable – seeing everything as good as it is. Making this hell of a relationship with yourself a little more bearable with yourself – that's all. All this fucking understanding everything is already final and perfect. Even the idea of final and perfection is bullshit. What kind of Absolute existence needs to be final and perfect? Only relative, little bullshit existence needs to be perfect.

The Absolute is what-it-is – perfect or imperfect. It doesn't care about being perfect at all or if it's still or not or silent. All this bullshit is a little plaster for your blood-running soul. [Laughter, clapping] When you really go to the nitty-gritty, everyone starts laughing. It's fun.

Q: David Carse really didn't want to write the book, but... [Laughter]

K: Aww... It gets worse. [Mocking] The angels were playing the harp and the blow-job of the angels made him write the book. [Laughter] If the angel would not have come at night and given him a blow job, he would not have written that job. He was so much asked by existence to write the bloody book.

So, why did he write the book?

Q: He had no choice...

K: He just wrote a book. So what? He was peeing in the *pisseur*. What's the difference between writing a book or peeing in a *pisseur*? No one asks why did you piss in the *pisseur*? [Laughter] Because there was pressure. I was drinking the night before so I had to piss in the morning. Why do you have to explain that he wrote the book because he had no choice?

I piss because I drink or I drink because I want to piss. [Laughter] Pissing is the best relaxation you can have and the best experience ever and for that you drink and you eat so that you can shit because it feels best when it comes out. [Laughter] Eating is just a nasty side-effect. [Laughing]

Q [Another visitor]: Now you're really going to the basics...

K: Everyone just eats for that. Then going to the toilet and being in heaven. It's better than any sex, especially for people with constipation.

So, why did he write the book?

Q [Another visitor]: He really didn't know what words to choose to explain what he wanted to say...

K: Then he should really be quiet. [Laughter] What's the problem in not writing a book? It's like I would write a book about how nice it is to go to the toilet. That's the best relaxation – perfect stillness in the toilet, sitting on the toilet.

Q [Another visitor]: I think he had a chemical reaction in the brain because earlier he was with the *shamans* right before the supposed event and that's still going on in the brain...

K: It's just a brain disease. It's just *ayawaska* running out. It's just a brain chemical bullshit. Every drug can give you all the spiritual experiences of all times. You just need the right drug and then later maybe the brain produces that drug. Then you see a different reality. In the seventies we did all kinds of things with Castaneda like *peyote, mescalito* and all of that.

It's all fantasm. Even seeing this is like a horror show. [Laughter] It's all a Muppet show.

Q: But he looks very happy now...

K: That's the worst thing. People end up in a mad house. No one goes there to kiss their feet because they have a happy face.

People who give hope that maybe by whatever they can get into that perfect state bullshit stillness and have a happy life after – that makes you suffer like hell. As you are already comparing yourself with that asshole [Laughter] and you don't know what he does at night or whether he has constipation in the toilet and is very happy with it. I mean it. All those who claim to have a happy relationship, happy marriage – they are all nasty. They are all lying anyway, they just want to make you jealous.

Q [Another visitor]: But some people are happier than others...

K: They are just less discomfortable and have less unhappiness – that's all. There are levels of discomfort and if someone is not in as much discomfort as you, you already call him happy. Because he only has twenty three hours of bad time and not twenty four. Who is comparing – who is happy and who is not? This happiness for sure is a temporary brain disease.

Q [Another visitor]: Look at Penelope Cruz, she's very happy...

K: Don't believe what people tell you. It's all Hollywood bullshit.

Q: I think she's really happy...

K: You think. You imagine. I tell you there's no happy person on earth, there's no happy being in the whole universe – never was, never will be. That's the best I can tell you because if there's no one who's happy, there's no one who's unhappy, both are bullshit.

But you now believe that you are a person and see Penelope who's happy.

Q: I'm happy for her...

K: Why should you be happy for her? Take care about yourself.

Q: I like people who are happy...

K: I like depressed people. They should all be depressed like hell because they believe that they're persons. The whole world should be depressed and I don't have to work on it, because they already are. Being a person is depression – from the beginning. It has to be like that. If there really would be happiness on earth, a paradise on earth, that really would be hell. If that really would be possible, that you can have a happy life, then I would shoot that one right away. If that really would be real, that he's happy – I would shoot that one – right away. Just out of compassion for all the other depressed ones. [Laughter]

That would be too much, if there really would be one who's happy. I think everyone would kill him. If they really would know that it's not impossible – they would kill him.

Q: She's happy with her husband and child...

K: Come on. You cannot be happy having a child. How can that happen? Even you regret that you have one and now you are jealous about another one who has a child.

Q: Yeah...

K: It's all discomfort, even being separated or being a person. You can only thank God and praise the Lord and Hallelujah – you can only experience discomfort and unhappiness because happiness can never be owned or experienced – Never ever. Thank God and praise the Lord – just-in-case.

Q: As all the Catholics do. They go to the church just-in-case...

K: Why not? You go to the pub and drink just-in-case it makes you happy. You eat just-in-case you may get satisfied. You can never get satisfied by anything. Thank God you cannot get satisfied by any experience. Imagine you could get satisfied by an experience of perfect stillness forever! That's called being dead.

I like Nisargadatta. He said – If you see the Reality as it is, you would run right away because you cannot bear the ocean of suffering which you are confronted with – in everything. No relative person can take it – never ever. But for what-you-are, there's simply no way out. You can only realize yourself in that experiences of war – levels of war with yourself in this passion or relation with what-you-are. You can only realize and experience yourself in separation. But it's for sure not the peace you are looking for and thank God you cannot experience peace or happiness. It will always be hell.

Q [Another visitor]: The moment you speak like that, I feel like jumping out of the window...

K: But nothing would happen here, it's very low. Next time we will speak on a high-rise building.

Q: It feels like I want to escape. It's fantastic but a part of me doesn't want to hear it...

K: I say it – it's not for you. I never speak to you anyway. For the person Shalaba – It never works. You will forget it anyway. The hope comes back when you step out of the door – all your ideas of happiness. And you will run for happiness. You will do your job. You will look for the next lover and will imagine that it makes you happy because that makes you take your ass off of bed in the morning.

You will always compare your life with the life of your neighbor or your best friend. Then you would think – Only if I were the wife of this guy or if I had this boyfriend or money. Maybe these tendencies dry out or maybe not. But you better be what-you-are, with and without it. If you depend on Shalaba's tendencies to be less or to get exhausted, you may wait forever.

Q: There are other times when this is so clear...

K: If you listen as Shalaba, it's unbearable. If you listen as what-you-are, it's wonderful. It's clarity itself – there's doubtless yes. There's a yes without even knowing why. But if you listen as the one who tries to understand what is being said, it becomes depression. It becomes too much and you cannot decide who's listening – the relative one listening with a relative ear or That what-you-are. You cannot decide.

But I'm talking to That one – ruthlessness talking to That one who has nothing to fear – the fearlessness. That's what you come for. Always after a while there's a little shift. You go from the relative understanding and suddenly there's a 'yes' without even knowing why. You don't even have to listen anymore. Then I can say whatever because then it's just okay. It doesn't even have to be okay.

But if you want to use your understanding, then you are in shit. That's why sometimes I talk so dirty and nasty because it becomes unbearable. For what you are it's just [Laughing] but for what you believe to be, it's unbearable – but I'm not interested in that one. Like UG [Krishnamurti] – Shit, shit, shit, talking these nasty things. Just creating the experience that you have to listen to it if you like it or not.

You have to realize yourself in likes and dislikes – equally. There will always be likes and dislikes, and it will never end. And you cannot decide that you can only have what you like to come to your ears and visions and senses. You have to sense whatever is there and however it comes. As what-you-are, it's no problem but for the one who has preferences, it's always hell. So, what to do?

So, you may jump now.

Q: Now, it's more like flying...

K: You want to fly now. In this case if there was an interest of talking to masses, I should talk differently. But I cannot. I would be so bored, I would kill myself right away that I have to listen to that. I would kill that right away. I cannot go one inch away from that ruthlessness because there's an unbelievable – whatever – what cannot be described. Nothing is more worth than being That and the rest you can just take away. It can be there or not – total carelessness.

Yet, if I care about you, how you feel about what I say, I would go out of it. Sometimes that happens. So, even that happens. But normally I don't speak that what the other person likes.

Q: But we always say what the other person wants to hear...

K: Normally, when I talk to my workers or with police, I do that. If I go to customs, I'm very polite, I lie. If they ask what are you here for? I'm just here to see the Grand Canyon. [Laughter] If I go to the butcher, I don't tell him you are not a butcher and there was no pig. I just want to have my sausage.

When it comes to talking about what-you-are, then there's no compromise, otherwise absolute compromise. I give a shit about people. But if you ask me about what-you-are, there's no compromise. If you really feel bad after what I said, I really give a shit. Imagine I would care about if one feels bad and may not come back! [Laughing] I would have many problems.

Q: Inside, I know what you say is right...

K: Shit. [Laughter] I'm right with whatever I say. I'm even right when I'm wrong. Whatever I say is wrong and I'm very right in that. In Bombay someone asked me – Why do you always have to be right? I said I have to be right and you have to be wrong, that's our agreement. [Laughter] You come as wrong and I come as right. Whatever I say is right and whatever you say is wrong.

Q [Another visitor]: Right! [Laughter]

K: I have to play the role of this one and you have to play the role of that one who's always wrong and even when you say something right, it's wrong because 'you' say it. But when I say something wrong or right, it doesn't matter because you want to defend what you say and I can say in one sentence, that and it's opposite, and give a shit about if it's right or wrong. So, it's neither right or wrong. But you have to be right and that makes you always wrong.

Q: Because 'I' have to be right?

K: Yeah and that makes you always wrong. [Laughter]

Q [Another visitor]: Someone asked me about what you talk about. It's very difficult to explain, so I had to give him the book...

K: That's what the books are for – Just read and be quiet.

Q: When I try to explain, they don't understand...

K: Why should they? [Laughter]

Q: With you it's very difficult to explain what happens... [Laughter]

K: You try to explain what even you didn't get. [Laughter] That doesn't work.

Q: I want to bring my friend here...

K: Don't do that. Many lost their friends after they brought them here. Some couples came together and went alone after a few minutes.

Q [Another visitor]: I lost a friend like that...

K: Bye, bye. I'm a good divorce agent. Sometimes even you lose enemies – if you are lucky. Why do you even try?

Q: Some people ask...

K: Then you tell them, go find it yourself, don't waste my time. Just be quiet.

Q [Another visitor]: It's very difficult to be quiet for me...

K: I know. [Laughter]

Q [Another visitor]: When my mother asks what am I doing here, I just say I'm going for yoga...

K: Just lie. For your peace, just lie. What's the problem with lying? You give the peace to the other one and yourself. Christa never lies...

Q [Another visitor]: I just thought I have never lied and now you say – lie...

K: You lie anyway. There's no one ever who said the truth. So, what's the problem with lying?

Q [Another visitor]: It's a sin...

K: You are a sinner anyway. Just by being born, you are a sinner.

Q [Another visitor]: To survive in this world, you have to tell relative lies...

K: Even to yourself all the time. When you wake up in the morning, you have to tell yourself That you-are. You say 'I Am' – you already lie. The moment you wake up, you lie. Then you look in the mirror and believe that it's you. You lie to yourself. You shave – a lie. You make up – a lie. Then you continue lying the whole day. What else can you do? Trying not to lie is a biggest lie. You dress – it's a lie. Everyone who doesn't want to lie should run naked – at least. [Laughter]

That's why the monks shave their head. They think that they're showing their real face. They don't want to hide something – Ha, ha, ha. Trying not to hide is hiding again. You hide the hiding. You show your face – I never use make-up.

God is a liar, the moment he knows himself – it's a lie. Why do you worry about your little day-to-day lies when even God is a liar? You are in good company all the time. You tell your mother – I love you – Ha, ha, ha. It's more like – I could kill you because you brought me to this bullshit world. No one likes mother or father. Just because someone tells you that she's your mother, you pretend to like.

Q: Many years ago, I used to talk like that. I used to tell my mother – I hate you because you gave me birth. But I was telling the truth.

K: Maybe it was another lie. I hate you all. That's a lie too but I hate you anyway. Every moment you're marketing yourself. You sell yourself – marketing your ideas, your body. Everyone is a businessman or woman always trying to sell. You want to sell something that you cannot even deliver but you want to have the money for it. [Laughter]

Men selling to a woman that 'I can satisfy you' – but they never can. And women selling that – I can make you happy, but it's the opposite – never. It's a crazy thing – selling, selling, buying, buying – until you die. Then you even worry what kind of coffin you end up in. Then you imagine that you want to be burnt because you don't trust your relatives, they may buy me a cheap coffin.

Q: Was there any disciple who succeeded his master?

K: No. Never was. There are many fake successors and success is still sucking on the tradition of their masters, on the lineage of their bullshit. There are rare ones like Nisargadatta who say – With me all the lineages end because that what is the Self has no lineage and no tradition and no history. Ramana said the same. They are really rare ones who say – No tradition of the Self and no masters and no disciples. That's the nature of a *satguru*.

Q: I don't trust people who have a lineage…

K: They are prostitutes who know that. They need a pimp behind them.

Q [Another visitor]: Some people say that you have to listen to your *satguru*…

K: You don't have to listen to it, you just have to be in the company. In That, there's no understanding. Good company means the absence of company. The absence of a teacher or a disciple. The absence of something to do or not to do – just to be That.

Q: What is *satguru*?

K: It is 'I' talking to the 'I'. It's not one who's happy talking to the one who's unhappy. It's not that there's one who knows and one who doesn't know. Even to make that special, is bullshit. Even making a standard of good company is bullshit. Even Ramana and Nisargadatta repeated it – If there's at all, it's good company. But you have to see good company as never-never because you're always in the company of what-you-are. Then you get pointers for That – that you cannot not have good company. All there is – is the Self and the good company is uninterrupted. It's not something that you can see as if 'there-is' and 'there-is-not'.

Good company is good company without one pointing out that one is better than something else. Even if someone's pointing that this is better, it is the same lie as everything else. That all the paradoxes appear and disappear and with it, sometimes you disappear.

Q [Another visitor]: Is baby in a good company?

K: No. Babies are the worst companies. Everyone falls in love with the innocent bullshit. Then you think you have to become like a baby. That's the worst company you can be in.

Q [Another visitor]: I don't like babies either...

K: Me neither. They need to be pampered and they stink and if you have no tits, they think you're worthless. I took care of a baby for four years. That was really hell. It really shows you the helplessness.

Q: Sometimes I wonder why don't I love them...

K: Watch out. After a while you fall in love with that innocence and you cannot help it. You will take care as much as you can. Don't worry. It's such a big trick of existence, making a baby so innocent. Looking at those innocent eyes and you fall in love with that innocence. Then you take care and you cry for it.

Good company is that there's no idea of good company and there's no need of understanding in good company. You want to understand what's a special good company. You want to make it a special thing again. But in good company, there's nothing special. All there is, is what-you-are. That's called good company. But not any special company – in the presence of a master or the presence of That.

It's not the presence of anything. It's the absence of any presence of separation or no-separation or whatever you can imagine. But that you cannot create because that's already there – never needs anything. That's already the case.

That's why they call them pointers. They're pointing to the fact – that what is life was always life and will always be life. It's always different but by all those differences it doesn't make it different and there's no company in life because life doesn't know any company. That's good company – when life is life, not knowing life, not knowing what is good or bad. If you make it special, that's bad company.

Q: Even when most of the people don't like their life, they don't want to die...

K: Everyone wants to be happy, they just have different techniques and happiness is the absence of the 'me'. They go to the pub and drink the 'me' away. They go to football just not to be confronted with themselves. Always escaping what they are. Even when you eat, you want to be happy. Everyone looks for satisfaction because there is one who's not satisfied. That's permanent – moment-by-moment. And there's no satisfaction even in this bloody bullshit perfect stillness. [Laughter] Don't believe one word of that.

October 6, 2012. Morning Talk.
Mallorca, Spain

There's no happiness in anything
...and that's the happy news

Q: I was thinking about taming the mind and it seems that there is no way…

K: You are here for instant success and not to make a detour of trying to control your thoughts and all of that. The taming of the bull is just being the bull not knowing any bull. It's same for the mind – not having the mind but being the mind. Then there's no mind anymore – was never there. That's taming the bull, totally – just by being what-you-are, which is mind, when there's mind but not having mind.

That's a total control and not a relative control of 'me' having a mind and controlling thoughts. I can just point that your natural state is the easiest – when there's mind, to be the mind but not having a mind. Then you're in absolute control of the whole totality because then you are the totality, whatever the totality means.

But whatever you do otherwise, trying to control it relatively is always futile. Because what you try to control, controls you. It's always a slave-master relationship.

Q: It's like not being identified with mind?

K: It's being absolute identified with the mind. Being the mind is absolute identification but not relatively more or less identified with something else – just by being That, what is mind because then you don't have mind and you don't know mind. Then you may call it intellect or wisdom. Then out of mind comes wisdom. Then there's crazy wisdom that you are mind but there's no direction of mind and no controller of mind.

So, it's very easy and natural to tame the bull – by being the bull. But the moment you have the bull, the bull controls you. The bull leaves you with a bloody nose.

Q: Does the same apply to desire?

K: Everything. When you are the desirer, the desiring and the desired, then you are That what-you-are. There's no desire anymore, there's no ownership of desire. There's still desire but – you are That – the desirer, desiring what can be desired. Then there's no harm in it, you cannot suffer about it when there's no separation in separation. Then there's an experience of separation but in nature there's no separation. Yes there is, but there's not. This is the end of suffering.

The same is with the mind. When you are mind, you cannot suffer about the mind. Only when you have mind, you suffer. It's all ownership. If you're a relative owner, you suffer. When you're the absolute owner, there's no possibility of suffering. And there's no bridge. There cannot be 'half' ownership or something. You are what-you-are – fine. If you are not – poor 'me'.

Q: Is it like a switch?

K: It's a shift without a shift. There's a shift without one who shifts. It's an absolute shift from shifting. It's the end of shift – that's the absolute shift. When you are time, there's no time. When you are separation, you don't know any separation. But when you are separated and you know separation, then you are in trouble all the time.

By not knowing what-you-are and what-you-are-not, it's all finished – instantly. Any moment you know yourself, you are fucked, because the moment you know yourself, you are separate from something else.

Q [Another visitor]: They say ignorance is bliss...

K: It's not ignorance. It's just an absence of one who knows or doesn't know. It's not like there's 'one' who doesn't know. There's not even 'one' who doesn't know. It's the absence of one who knows and the absence of one who doesn't know. It's even the absence of absence which is the absence of absence and the absence of presence, presence-absence-absence-presence-absence...

You cannot follow that. No one can ever reach that. That's the beauty of it – unattainable. You will never attain that.

Q: You say everything has happened already...

K: It's already there...

Q: The 'A-ha' moment?

K: That's already there too...

Q: Can you see that in the horoscope?

K: Maybe, maybe not. This moment was already written.

Q: It would be interesting when this moment happens...

K: It never happens because it's not in time. You cannot find it in time, so you cannot make a horoscope out of it. Otherwise you make it a future event. If 'A-ha' happened in time, it would be gone by time. The 'A-ha' is never-never. The split-second is not what you can place in time.

It's like the heart breaks and the connection with the ownership drops – absolutely. That's the heart-break. The heart knot breaks and then there was not even 'one' before. The heart knot breaks because you see that you are with and without it and you will never break it because that's the way you realize yourself. That there never will be any heart break – that breaks your heart because the heart what can be broken, will always fix itself and then you continue the whole story.

You can never get rid of the phantom. That's breaking the heart. You have to realize yourself first as a realizer – that's already the phantom. The first false 'I' – you cannot avoid. It will always be there. That breaks your hope totally and your imaginary future ideas that in the horoscope you can see when your 'A-ha' will be. It will never be your 'A-ha'. It's not a personal event – cannot be. Actually every night when you go to sleep, it's like 'A-ha'. But there's no one left.

What-you-are is with and without it anyway – the presence or absence of the phantom idea. We're talking about Buddha's end of suffering. Even Vashistha says – It's most easy but you cannot do it. You can only 'be' it but you cannot 'become it'. You cannot attain it, under any circumstance. On the other hand, you cannot not be it. So, be that what doesn't need to know itself to be itself. That what needs to know itself – is always the phantom – unreal and it will always stay unreal.

Q [Another visitor]: Sometimes this is just too hard and I want to escape. But I can't...

K: No escape.

Q: What to do?

K: It's fun. It's peaceful. If you can stay in that no-escape, it's all fine. Let the phantom be. That's the essence of it, you cannot get out where you are not in. How to get out where you are not in? And how to change a dream which you are not even in?

Q [Another visitor]: It's good to know that there's nothing to change...

K: There's a lot to change but it will not change anything.

Q [Another visitor]: We wake up in the morning and feel that things are not right...

K: That's normal.

Q: Is that natural?

K: It's more than natural. [Laughter] You wake up – wrong. The first thing is – Shit, here I am again.

Q: Then the next thing is trying to make it different...

K: To make gold out of shit.

Q: Trying to make it better...

K: Yeah. That's trying to make gold out of shit. You become an alchemist – instantly. That's natural. Out of love for yourself you want to make your beloved comfortable. You wake up in discomfort of sensational ownership and that's discomfort.

Q: Is it possible to change that?

K: No. That will always be the case.

Q: Is it not possible to come to a place of...?

K: Temporarily. But the moment you wake up, you are already in discomfort. Waking up on a bed is already discomfort. Then trying to make it better, makes it worse. You cannot change that. That's your little love affair with your relative life and you are surrounded by that – intention to be happy or making it more comfortable for what-you-are.

And the biggest comfort would be without the 'one' who could be in discomfort. So, you're looking for the end of the 'me'. Because without 'me' there would be no discomfort. There's a knowledge – you know that without a 'me', you would be fine. So, you do everything that you can do to end the 'me' because the 'me' means suffering – discomfort – me-sery.

Q: And the ending of the ownership?

K: That's 'me'. The 'me' means ownership. The sensational ownership – my body, my life, my story. It's always a relative ownership story. That cannot go. It always will be different, a different flavor of the owner. Ownership can have different kinds of flavors but it will always be relative ownership. There's no satisfaction in it. There's no comfort, no satisfaction that you look for. Then there's already a seed to get out of it – instantly.

You want to end it by having coffee, by going to the toilet, doing make-up. You want to at least make it bearable. But it's not bearable – never was. The whole humanity – they go to pubs and drink, they go to football games or watch television. These are all techniques to make the discomfort less, to make it more bearable. Everything what is done in the whole universe, is with the intention of happiness, trying to end discomfort. Or looking for harmony which will never be there in the relative experience – cannot be.

There will never be the harmony that you are looking for when there's two. When there's you and the universe, when there's you and something else. There can only be fake harmony that you have to fight for. That's a fake peace. It's a ceasefire for a while, then you start shooting again. But then everyone promises peace and everyone fights for it. Everyone fights for peace and that's called war because everyone has a different idea of peace.

Everyone has a different religion and a different God which means a different idea of happiness or reality and then everyone fights for that truth or reality against everyone – My truth is the only true truth and my religion is the only true religion. That's the reason of all the wars in this world, between neighbors and countries. Even in marriages. One says – I see it this way and my reference point is true. It has to be like this and the other one says the same. And both are true.

Q: Is it possible to drop that?

K: No. There's no need. Maybe one in a billion can drop it but what does that mean when the rest of humanity is still fighting and only one is not? When one woke up from it? What does that mean? Then he takes it personally that he is not fighting anymore – I am in peace with myself. Even to say that is already a joke – I am in peace with myself... Ha..ha..ha.. I don't fight anymore. Sound's good – that's all.

What is the idea of *bodhisattvas*? They just continue because there's no way out. They see that there will always be beings and consciousness in one or the other case will fight. If in one case it ends, what about all the other cases? In this world of realization, there will always be war. And if in one case the war stops, who cares? It's a temporary stopping because that what can stop is always dangerous because it can start again. Even in that case.

There's always a tolerance limit even for a master that is awakened from his so-called illusory 'I'. Then suddenly it's back again – the ego return. It has happened so many times. There will always be a big camel that steps over your feet and suddenly the 'no me' is a 'double me'. Or when someone comes and doubts him, you can see how he fights for his 'no me'. Even that becomes a religion. That there's 'no me', that there's no one. All the neo-advaita guys fight for that there's no one.

What did Jesus talk about in the Thomas gospel? When there's world, there will always be war. When there's two, when there's father and son, the son will kill the father. There will never be any end to it. Out of Jesus, the embodiment of love, he became Christ. Even he changed to a different person.

One tree fights against another tree, one blade of grass fights against another blade of grass for sun. Even in nature you can only see fighting for survival, for getting the best. The roots of one tree go deeper and suck water from the other tree without caring that the other tree is dying. It's same as two people fighting for a piece of land or woman. Everything is stupid.

Q: So, the development of consciousness is another nice illusion?

K: Sounds good – evolution. For me it's evil-lution because it's an evil idea. That there has to be a transformation of consciousness. That consciousness gets to a higher level. That only puts consciousness down and makes it a bullshit consciousness because there's a consciousness that needs to transform, that needs to evolve in itself to become what-it-is? What kind of consciousness is that which needs to change?

Q: In an absolute way it doesn't need an evolution...

K: And in the relative way?

Q: There are all kinds of levels...

K: What kinds of levels are that? Shit, shit, shit – levels of shit.

Q: Higher shit sounds better...

K: Only for eunuchs [you knocks]. You knock and I knock and nobody opens. [Laughter]

Q [Another visitor]: Consciousness doesn't evolve but what about human consciousness?

K: What an idea that humans have consciousness! Imagine humans would have consciousness. Does consciousness have humans or humans have consciousness? That's the main question. Who owns whom? I'm serious.

Q: Consciousness owns humans...

K: Consciousness owns humans and by playing human doesn't become human. Consciousness plays stupid but it doesn't become stupid. Knowledge plays ignorance but it doesn't become ignorant by that. So, nothing happens. It plays humans – so what? Show me the evolution of humanity. They just have different kinds of sticks to beat the other one up, different techniques. Where's the evolution? Where's civilization? Show me. It's still the stone-age same brain.

Q: There seems to be a kind of evolution in the animal world...

K: There's a change but I don't call it evolution.

Q: The fact that humans have evolved in the first place...

K: From one cell to many cells? Do you think that's higher? Do you think elephants have the highest evolution because they have more cells in their body?

Q: Humans are obviously the highest form of evolution...

K: Evil-lution – Yes. That's really evil-lution, what people can do to people. The science of war and what they can destroy now.

Q: It is said that you need to have a human body in order to...

K: Who said that? One having a human body who claims that he made it. Who else would claim that?

Q: Shankaracharya...

K: Maybe he meant that you have to realize yourself even as a human – worse as it is. It's the worst incarnation, being a human. Nothing is worse than the fact that you have to be a human. That you have to reflect and need to have a history and you have to remember your childhood. Is that an evolution? Look at a fly, that's the end of evolution – one day life. You wake up in morning and by night – bye, bye. That's the whole life time of a fly.

What did humanity reach? Electricity? Computers? Television?

Q: Great art...

K: Where will it be in few thousand years? Who will remember? So, that's nothing reached because it will be gone. It's already dead. There's nothing what's worth keeping. It will be gone anyway. The next sip of coffee is as worth as the biggest art on earth. Just enjoy it and forget it.

Q [Another visitor]: This year in 2012...

K: Yeah. The world goes down.

Q: There will be a global transformation...

K: Yeah. That means the world goes down. [Laughter] Then there's no time and no world anymore. But the bad thing is three months ago they found the next plate. So, we have a few thousand years more. And they found it just a few meters deeper. For years there were movies about the end of the world and now they find a second plate.

So, all the Eckhart Tolle's and all the New Earth's have to wait a bit longer. [Laughter] It's not 'now', it will be later. [Laughter]

Q: More suffering?

K: There's never more or less suffering. But it sounds good. Many books were written about it and a lot of money was made by that idea. We had this a few times already. The millennium, in 1993 there were light circles. In the seventies there was transcendental meditation. Maharishi wishy-washy was promising the whole change of humanity. Now it's the oneness university.

Hope is best to sell. It's good business. If everyone would say what I say then... [Laughter]

Q: Money?

K: Money is fun.

Q: How to balance between too little and too much?

K: There's never enough money. [Laughter] It doesn't harm to have more money. If you have more and more millions, but after the first one it makes no difference. Money is neutral, money is just money. I like money. It doesn't harm, it doesn't bring anything and doesn't take anything. It doesn't bring you happiness and doesn't take away your suffering. It's just money. People always blame it for some reason. It's not the money, it's their greed. The idea of what they can buy with it or how much they need. Money is like oxygen, needed for breathing.

Q: It's just for needs?

K: No. It comes when it comes and when not, it doesn't come. Mostly you have to work for it but some people don't have to work. It comes from heritage. They're even more fucked. [Pointing to a visitor] Like he gets money for not working. [Laughter]

Q [Another visitor]: What about people who need money and don't have enough?

K: Even the richest person doesn't have enough. He will find a reason that he needs more. Even Bill Gates doesn't have enough, he has so many plans of saving the world. He needs more money. It's never enough.

Q: Too much money is harmful...

K: Yeah. Imagine there's enough money then no one would work anymore. Everyone would die. You have to create a need so that people do something. That's the trick. You need a pressure or need so that something happens. They think, I need that television so I have to work. For the basic things like water and bread there would always be enough.

But for those special needs – what you think makes you happy – the new car, the television, the apartment, sofa, fridge, then you're in trouble. That makes you work hard. Because your neighbor has a new car, you need one or the neighbors wife has new clothes, your wife needs it too. There's a competition running. It's not the money that's bad, it's the competition between people.

But even that's natural. It's like a sport. Everyone feels insecure and thinks that when I gather this and that, I would be more secure. More money is more insurance – I don't have to worry so much. It's all about fear, fear that you would not survive without money. All of that is being insecure.

Q: The richest people in the world also have fear?

K: They fear to lose it. There's no insurance in anything. Then you have to buy a new liver from Turkey like Angelina Jolie. It seems like when you have money, you have to live longer. That's not so good. [Laughter] You buy a new heart, new liver. It's like hell – everywhere.

If you have money, you worry. If you don't have money, you worry. You worry anyway. It's like having a girlfriend or no girlfriend. If you have no girlfriend, you worry. If you have one, you worry even more. [Laughter] There's no end of worries. When you wake up in the morning, you start worrying for different things.

When you have money, you worry whether your wife really loves you or your money. [Laughter] Then you're really fucked – Why does my wife fuck with me? For my money or my dick? [Laughter] Then you're really insecure – Why does she smile at me? Because I pay her expenses or because she really likes me? You can never be sure. If you have no money and a girlfriend, you can be a bit more sure that she likes something else, but still not you.

I tell you, you are fucked from the beginning. It's a total fuck-up the moment you're born. You can never be sure. Why does my mother like me? I don't even like myself. Relation-shit – Hell, everywhere. All just for security – I don't want to be alone, someone takes care of me.

Q: Don't you think wall street is an ugly place?

K: It's the most ugly place. That's why they have to wear nice suits and shoes. [Laughter]

Q [Another visitor]: Sometimes it's difficult to get things out of the system when they go deep at a younger age...

K: It's imprinted like a conditioning you cannot dissolve, like a *karmic* knot. Then you want to solve it because you think that blocks me.

Q: We look for conformation in the world with our conditioning of the past...

K: Sometimes you prepare for the future that really happens and sometimes not. It's like you prepare for death and when it happens, it doesn't happen because it doesn't kill you. It's amazing. But you prepare yourself for the whole life, for that moment of death and nothing happens... oops. Shit!

Kubler Ross wrote about near death experiences and was always working on it. She had years of cancer and suffering, she really could not take it. But for forty years, she was working with people and writing books and preparing herself for dying. But when it happened to her, she was totally unprepared. She was in complete despair and suffering. She did many sweat lodges with *shamans* and she was more than prepared. But when it really happened... No!

Q: My brother-in-law died few days back and I was thinking if you subscribe to the idea that a soul is reincarnated?

K: Maybe. Just like you take your soul to the next morning. It's the same. You go to bed in the deep-deep absence. Then in the morning the soul wakes up again. It's like a reincarnation. It seems like a similar functioning that a 'me' wakes up again. Maybe its the same when death happens. Maybe it's like a deep-deep sleep night and then waking up in another form. Who knows?

But that doesn't mean that there's one who's incarnated now. You can say it's like a genetic cluster that's incarnated in something else. But right now I wouldn't say that is an incarnation of a 'you'. It's just a label or a mask of a genetic functioning of a past that just continues in something else. Like the Dalai Lama, fourteen times now – can happen. Why not? Everything is possible in this dream. But still there's no one incarnated. No one is ever born.

But this genetic cluster and energy can go on. It seems like a memory cluster of something and then it goes into the next form. That I can see. Sometimes I talk to someone and I see many forms in front of me, changing faces. Just like a cluster of memory effects presenting itself in that form. But I wouldn't say it's now a reincarnation from whatever. But sometimes you see all the faces in front of you – always shifting. Doesn't mean there's one who's incarnated. It's just consciousness showing lineage of memories and not one individual soul, that's incarnated again and again. Doesn't happen.

It's always the Absolute soul that shows itself in different forms. Sometimes in lineages and sometimes random. Everything is possible. So, there's reincarnation, but not for any 'one'. It's always a reincarnation of consciousness in forms – again and again. As I said, sometimes in lineages a functioning happens again in similar tendencies waking up in that particular form.

Even when you remember yourself as a child or something in

between, it's always someone different wakes up. It's never the same. So, you cannot find any specific 'I' which is very stable. It's always transforming. Never the same one wakes up. Is that evolution?

Q: I have a dual reaction to it because of the strong sense of sympathy that I feel for my brother-in-law...

K: You didn't feel for him. You had a sense of sympathy for your sister. You only experience for the leftovers, who suffer – they are left over when someone went. Who's more pitiful? The one who is dead or the one who has lost someone? I don't know.

No one grieves for the one who's dead – never. You're always grieving for yourself or your leftover family. Everyone is actually unhappy that he's not the one who died. Then you imagine how it would be when you would die. Maybe you're jealous of the dead person. Why him, not me?

Q [Another visitor]: Ramana just laid down his life when he was fifteen...

K: He imagined what it would be to die. But he didn't die. He went through all the experiences of dying but in none of those experiences what-he-was could die. The body could die, the ideas of spirit could die. All what you can imagine could die but still you are what-you-are. You are Absolute, without all of that you can experience – even without the experiencer you-are. And that cannot die because That was never born. That's what he experienced.

Your nature is inspite of everything what-it-is. That's the death experience. Everything can die but what-you-are cannot by any means die by any experience. As you are not born in the experience of birth because you are already there before the two liquids meet, you are already there before you have a mask, a persona. You would be afterwards what-you-are. There's no one who's born. How can there be someone to die when in the first place there was no one born?

Find first who's born now. Can you show me anyone who's

born? Show me one. You can show me pieces of meat but you cannot show me what-you-are. It cannot be found in anything. Flesh comes in a flash and in a flash it goes. Nothing is lost when someone dies. Nothing is gained if a baby is born. Life doesn't become more or less when there's more or less – something more or less. Seven billion people now. But what does it mean? Infinite supply, never enough.

[Mocking] This precious body – my beloved, my arthritis – the disease. It always needs an insurance, a house, a bed to sleep upon. Always needs something, this little monster.

People are crazy from the beginning. What people do to people – even the devil cannot be so inventive. These nasty things – that you even do to yourself.

Q [Another visitor]: Why are we here?

K: I have no idea. Why not?

Q [Another visitor]: I was thinking about what you said about reincarnation and I realize how strong we have this fear about continuity...

K: Fear that something stops. Then you want to make sure that at least your soul continues.

Q: All the narratives that we create in our life just for a historical continuity...

K: The archaeologists go digging into the earth to find some artifacts and are happy if they find something and know how people lived at that time. Just totally fixed on that bullshit – on the past. If I would be a dictator I would make these people work in a factory so that people have at least something to eat. [Laughter]

Q: I'm still attached to the idea of evil-lution...

K: Everyone is. Everyone who comes here thinks that by whatever they do, whatever they understand, they can get closer to their nature or to happiness or peace, whatever their goal is. That's called evolution – more real, nicer experiences, more calm. Like marriage, people try for fifty years to understand their wife. But the moment the husband understands his wife, he gets divorced. [Laughter]

Q: At the same time the world as we know seems to be a product of the past...

K: Or the future demand. So that the future can be as the future is, the present moment has to be as it is. It's more or less a product of future and past. It's a total demand of future and past so that it is like it is. Your action now leads to the future which is already there. What you want now makes sure that the future is as it is. It's not your decision. The future decides it already. You can even say that the last moment was the infinite future as their future ends. [Clapping] This is the beginning and end of everything. The future ends with now.

Q [Another visitor]: I see it the other way round. Like when you play billiards, you hit the ball and because of that it goes to the hole. Is that how life works?

K: Maybe the ball had to go to the hole and that's why you made that exact angle.

Q: That seems complicated...

K: Then just stay with your concept,.I don't want to make it complicated for you. I just say that you can say the future demands or the past demands – both is bullshit. There's no demand in anything. It's just as it is. It's a fixed block of what-it-is. When *brahman* wakes up, everything is just there. Just by waking up, everything is already fixed. The Absolute Reality waking up to the Absolute realization, there's nothing coming and nothing going in that. There are many experiences but nothing happens because everything is – forever – eternal now, infinite now.

Nothing is added and nothing can be taken away and nothing happens in That. There's no birth and no death in That. There are many experiences but even they are infinite. This is like a *deja vu* from all the previous times because this moment never comes and never goes. That's the *akashic* records – it's always repeating again and again, the very same thing. An unmovable block of realization.

This moment in it's nature contains the whole future and past of all possibilities. This moment is the source of all the futures and pasts. It's already there.

Q: You sound like Eckhart Tolle – The Power of Now...

K: No. That's not the power of now. He makes it as an advantage that – you are in the now. No. It's not an advantage, it is as it is – the infinite now. He calls it 'now' but he forgets to call it the infinite now.

The quantum physics are quite close. They say that if one particle knows something, the particle in the most distant place in the universe also knows it instantly. There's knowledge without time. There's no distance in Reality. If one knows, the entire universe knows. There's no here or there, so there's no difference.

Q [Another visitor]: Does the future demands an effort to be itself?

K: No. The effort happens so that the future can be already as future is. All the actions or whatever happens now don't create the future, the future creates the action now. You cannot take one out of the other, both are interrelated. If you think that by your doing you can alter the future, then you become a doer and then you feel responsible for your actions. But if the future demands the action now, you cannot take it personal. That's quite different. Then it cannot be your action and if it's not your action, you don't have to justify what you have not done.

If you understand that, it's quite relaxing. But even that depends on your understanding. There are many possible ways to reach a relative peace. But even by the wisdom of scientific conclusions, you cannot attain the peace that you're really longing for. It can only be relative because it demands understanding. It demands some insights and that is always relative. It's all part of the dream of ignorance.

The deepest understanding of all times cannot deliver anything – even if you would be Einstein or someone. That's why it's called relativity terror-rey[theory]. Then you have to prove your terror-rey. You're in a permanent terror of proving your point.

Be the laziest of the laziest you are because that's your fucking nature. That has never done anything and by nature never needs to know anything to be what-it-is. And the rest would always be a scientific fiction which will never lead to any end. So, you can know the whole universe and you will still be a stupid asshole.

Q [Another visitor]: They found out that there are particles that go faster than the speed of light...

K: No. It cannot go faster than light, it was a measuring mistake. Light has no speed, it's silence.

Q: But it has been measured...

K: No. You cannot measure light. Einstein was an idiot. [Laughter] I mean it. Light cannot be measured because that what you can measure is a reflection of light. But it's not light. It's like light of Shiva – How can you measure it? Where's the speed of the light of Shiva? That's silence. When it wakes up, there's an absolute speed and absolute speed means silence. It's everywhere and it's already there where it started instantly. That's the absolute speed. It's the absolute speed which is silence – just a solid block of silence. Can you imagine the nature of light? It goes by absolute speed and it's already there, where it starts – just by waking up.

The quantum physicists have a glimpse of it. That there's no difference here and there because there's no time in between and there's no speed. The absolute speed or the speed of light means there's absolutely no movement.

Q [Another visitor]: In sometime they would have another theory...

K: That's called the evolution of ignorance – changing point of views. That can only be in relative. So what? But the light of Shiva is never relative because there's only the light of Shiva as there's only Shiva. And there cannot be any speed of Shiva because speed can only happen when you can measure it. You can never measure the light of Shiva – this absolute that what is the light.

Q [Another visitor]: But they measured the phenomenon of light...

K: That's not light. Light is energy. How can you measure energy? You can only measure the results of that energy – like electricity. They can't even explain what is electricity. They didn't find matter. They can just measure a reaction of a reaction but not That what is the action. They were looking for matter and energy but they could not find it. You cannot find energy you can only measure the reaction of that energy but not the action. So what do the scientists know? Nothing.

In India *Brahma* and Vishnu wanted to find the end of the light of Shiva. Vishnu said it could not be found and *Brahma* was cheating saying that he found the end of light. Scientists are always cheating.

Q [Another visitor]: Is it that the formless can only be known in forms?

K: The ultimate can only know itself in something relative as the ultimate cannot know the ultimate. The Absolute never knows the Absolute because for knowing, it needs two. So, it imagines a dream of separation to know different aspects of what-it-is but it will never know its nature. It always has to divide itself as subject-object to know itself. But it will never know its nature. For sure not in any relative way. Absolutely you know that 'you are'. No one can take it away and no one can give it to you. You know that 'you are'.

What was the basic of Ramakrishna's teaching? Even to say – I don't know, you have to know. That even to say – I am not, you have to be. That you can make any statement, before the one who makes this statement, has to be that what can make a statement. Before there can be a relative knower, That what is knowledge has to be there. For even an experience of an experiencer, that what is in nature experiencer has to be – That what-it-is.

You always forget That what is omnipresent, which has no presence, which is the presence without which no relative presence could be. And I can only point it, moment-by-moment; without That 'you are', without That knowledge 'you are', there cannot be the slightest of experience or no-experience at all. But you always forget That. You always give attention to the fleeting shadow world but never to That which allows the shadow world to be, which is realizing itself as shadows.

Without the light 'you are', you cannot experience the relative light of the experience of light. So, the light of Shiva that you can experience, is not Shiva. The nature of light, will never know light. And That what you can know as light is already a reflection of the light. Awareness is already a reflection of That what-you-are. What-you-are is inspite the presence or absence of awareness, not because. There is awareness because 'you are' but 'you are' not because awareness is.

So, what is there to fear from? You are even inspite of awareness. In spite of the light of Shiva, you are That what-you-are. That you can call *Parabrahman* – the Absolute dreamer – which is with and without the dream. The dream starts with awareness and space and whatever comes out of That space. But inspite of it, with and without the experience of awareness – you are. This omnipresence, which is in the absence or presence of anything what-it-is, That is the Absolute because there's no second to That.

That you can call Reality that starts to realize itself as a realizer, as awareness. It becomes a creator, creating what can be created. But with and without the creator – you are. So, you are not the creator, not the creation and there's nothing to create. That you can never know, but you are – That. That is not something you can attain by awareness. How can you attain that by awareness which is already there without the awareness? What an idea!

You make yourself depend on the reflection of yourself to exist. That's the ignorance. That you imagine that you have to be aware to exist. That you have to know yourself or be conscious to exist. No! You are with and without the bloody consciousness – what-you-are. Consciousness needs you but you don't need consciousness. Without you being That what-you-are, there would not be even consciousness. And you make yourself a slave of your own reflection. What came into your bloody – whatever it is? [Laughing]

What a joke! Isn't it a joke? The almighty takes himself as if it's depending on an idea – on a reflection of itself. You become a slave of an idea. But shit happens! You fall in love with an asshole you think you are. [Laughter] Then because you became one, you believe in other assholes and then it stinks. [Laughter] Then it really starts stinking because there are so many assholes. Different types of assholes – vegetarian assholes, meat eating assholes – disgusting. [Laughter]

Then it's like [Jean-Paul] Sartre – The other is hell. But there are only others because there is one. So many holes but where is the ass? You are the ass and you have many holes.

Q [Another visitor]: Can you speak about breaking the Heart knot?

K: The breaking of the Heart knot is splitting the second. When you are That what is realizing itself, then in split second you see that you are the origin of awareness. You are not the product of awareness, awareness is a product of you. Since awareness is a product of you and whatever comes out of awareness, this breaks all your ideas of future or past because you cannot escape what-you-are. The heart knot is just a hope that one day you can escape this hell.

But you cannot escape the hell, which is a realization of what-you-are. That breaks your fucking heart. Before you always fuck around with ideas that one day you will make it and get out of this mess. No, this is your absolute mess. You are the most messy, the absolute messy guy who's messing around with himself forever.

The relative heart that you believed in – the love affair – means that one day you would know your beloved. Then this idea drops totally because you will never know That what is realizing itself. Whatever you know as realizing itself, will always be relative and will never show what-you-are. The love affair with yourself stops totally, that's like the heart knot breaks. You can never know your beloved and you will never be happy.

That's not so bad because then peace is – as it always was. Because what-you-are is only the hope for happiness which makes you so stupid to look for an escape. And you will never be happy – never ever. There's no happiness, in anything. That's the happy news. No one will ever be happy. There was never anyone who was happy and there will never be anyone who will be happy.

Whatever you can experience, is discomfort and hell. Happiness cannot be experienced. [Laughing] Knowledge cannot be experienced – can never be known by anyone, not even by yourself. Peace can never be known by anyone – not even yourself. There will never be any peace. No happiness, no peace, no satisfaction, no truth can be experienced.

Q [Another visitor]: But you experience few moments of happiness in life?

K: Never. Never ever anyone experienced happiness. What many people call happiness is the absence of the 'me'. If you have sex, in the orgasmic experience there's an absence of the 'me' – the sufferer. They call that happiness. But that's a happiness that depends on the absence of the 'me'. That's a relative happiness. That's not the happiness I'm talking about. The relative happiness you can reach but that depends on the absence of the one who is unhappy. I'm not talking about that 'depending' happiness.

That is a relative happiness that depends on the absence of the one who is not happy. That you can experience, that's why people fuck around like hell. People go to the bar and drink themselves away. You take every drink until no one is there anymore, until you feel the absence of the 'me'. Then you are drunk and happy but then you have a hangover next day. The 'me' comes back fresh and strong. Then you need more drinks, more drugs.

Q: When I'm in the field alone and working...

K: In that case, the working is the drug. You work yourself away. Some meditate themselves away. But it's all a technique to create an absence. Everyone has a different technique of being absent – going to kitchen, gardening, nature walk or marathon. Some run marathon until they reach a dead point. Then the last ten kilometers no one runs. They call it trance of running. Some climb the mountains and while climbing the climber drops at one point and climbing remains.

By whatever effort – you can go to the temporary absence. As every night by nature you fall asleep and there's a temporary absence of the 'me'. Then if you didn't have a dream, you say – It must have been good. It was very nice. I don't know what was there but it was good because there was nothing happening. You cannot remember and that's a good sign of absence. The rest is always presence and that's hell because you need both to make a difference.

Q: So, deep-deep sleep is happiness?

K: Deep-deep sleep is not happiness. In deep-deep sleep you are that happiness without the experience of the one who is happy or unhappy. At first you experience the unhappy one and then by effort, you come to the absence of the unhappy one. That you call happiness. Then you define – this is happiness and that is unhappiness. Then in deep-deep sleep, you are That what is your nature, you can call it happiness itself which is inspite of the presence or absence of the one who is happy or unhappy – what-it-is. But you cannot say what happened. There was even no one who was 'not'. That's more the nature of – what-you-are. The happiness that's inspite.

And to be That now, is what-you-are. It's not an experience. But you have to experience 'one' who is sometimes happy and sometimes not. That 'one' always has to work for his little happiness. It has to do something or needs some special circumstance where he can be absent or the attention has to be so occupied that he gets lost. Or you have to be in the 'now' all the time. Sounds very hard!

You realize yourself as happy or unhappy – heaven and hell. Absence is heaven and presence is hell. 'Me' is hell and absence of 'me' is heaven and that will always be the case. It's like you realize yourself in light and darkness – in presence and absence. In good and bad. It always comes with polarities and it will always be like that.

You think that after the moment of enlightenment, you will always be happy – for now and forever. [Laughing] For that you really work hard, meditate and try to understand everything, you go to transcendental meditation. But you would never reach that point. And if one got established at that point, in the temporary screen-like presence where all the projections are dancing, what about the rest? Maybe one reaches and really works so that he doesn't move one inch from it. He really has to be quiet. It's a depending presence of absence because you have to be quiet for it. You really have to not move. If you move an inch, everything is lost again.

Any intention coming from there for the world, falling in love with something, you lose again what was before. That's the Tao teaching. You can reach the *samadhi* of the presence of awareness which is like a screen where the world dances upon. But sooner or later you have to come back to the market place if you like it or not. You can stay there for ages, for thousands of years, but you have to come back.

And when you are back in the market, you are as thirsty as before – no difference. Because there was no time in between. You just ordered a drink and went to thousands of years of *samadhi*. When you come back, you have to drink the next sip from that drink. That's the problem. There was no times and when you come back, there will be the same next moment. And you thought you made it? No. When you come back, you have to drink the next bloody drink.

Q [Another visitor]: What is the difference between the *samadhi* and the A-ha moment?

K: The *samadhi* of awareness is a personal *samadhi*. You still take it personally that you are the screen where nothing happens and the world is different from what-you-are. There are projects but you are established in awareness. But that's still a personal awareness. The thirst for yourself cannot be stopped by that personal awareness. You always come back and you are as thirsty as before.

Q: Can I know that it's only a *samadhi*?

K: Many masters talk about it. They know and they claim that they're established in That. Then they tell you, you will be better off, if you follow me. I can teach you to reach that place. So, they give you a reference point where they claim to be established in. They speak from there and I believe them. It's authentic. But it's a reference point and any reference point is a relative one. Then they tell you that it's an advantage. Yes, it is an advantage. I believe it but a relative advantage of a personal advantage. If you are looking for that, go for it.

But I sit here and tell you That the absolute advantage – not needing any advantage, is your nature. And just by being what-you-are, nothing has to be done. But if you are interested in a personal advantage, then you go to someone who can give you that. I have no interest in that.

My absolute interest is [small mischievous pause] I have no idea! [Laughter]

Q: Can you see someone stuck in *samadhi*?

K: Yeah. Sometimes people come as awareness and the whole space is filled with light. It's quite energetic. When I see them it's all golden light. Some come with silver light as I Amness. The whole space becomes silver.

Q: What do you do then?

K: I don't have to do anything. I just ask them – Why do you come to me?

Q: Is it good to have a golden light?

K: From a personal point of view you can say there's an evolution from a personal body to spirit and to the awareness. So, from the personal point of view, it's better than this body. But it needs one who discriminates. Yes, it's better in a relative world and if you are interested in that, by all means go for it but leave me alone.

Q: Is it necessary to go through *samadhi*?

K: If you want to go through that, yes. If you listen to me, maybe not.

Q [Another visitor]: But for you, it went that way?

K: Now he wants to make a rule out of it. No one knows. For some, they have to go through all the bullshit and some don't. It doesn't matter if you go or not. It will happen anyway but not because of someone's effort. It happens as everything else happens – by itself. And not if one has it or not. Don't take it personally and don't make it a Karl's story or your story. You are so bloody fixed in your personal story and you want to compare your story with the story of someone else – bullshit.

Then you also want to make a point that for me it was the same. Why should I not go through it? You always look for excuses so that you remain stupid. You say – You were once stupid too so why should I not be stupid? [Laughter] If you want to make a detour to the whole universe and go through roller-coaster rides – why not?

But then first you have to milk cows. [Laughter] If you want to repeat the 'Karl's story', you have to be born with the same grandmother. Then every bloody moment you have to repeat and not just few moments. You need a total new life from the beginning if you say – it has to be like that. You have to be like Ramana, but you are not fifteen anymore, so it's too late. [Laughter] Everyone wants to be like Ramana but not the way his life went.

It's anyway too late for everybody here. Only the dog can make it. [Laughter]

Q [Another visitor]: So, all the spiritual experiences are not necessary?

K: They are necessary. You cannot miss them. Because you are That what-you-cannot-not-be, you have to realize yourself in all that bullshit. You cannot miss one of it.

Q: But I understood that we don't have to do anything? [Laughter]

K: You didn't understand anything. How can you understand anything correctly? Every fucking understanding is a misunderstanding. And repeating it doesn't make it better. Especially repeating something what you have not understood at all.

Q: That's what I mean...

K: There's a 'me' in it. I me-an. You want to have something what you can never own. But you want to put it in your bloody brain and take it home.

Q [Another visitor]: If one is full of light...

K: He's not full of light, he just has a reference point of light. He is a 'fool' of light and not full of light.

Q: Is that a temporary state?

K: It has to be since he entered that state. He landed in that and he will depart from there. If he's unlucky, he departs to the first again where he came from. When he's lucky, by accident he stumbles into the beyond. But Jesus had to be crucified for that and no one is ready for crucification. When I ask everyone – Are you ready to be crucified? You want to have the opposite. Everyone who went there had to be crucified to the eye of the needle.

Q: But that's death!

K: It's not death. It's an experience of the absence but you're still present. You cannot experience death. That's the point. Because you can experience that what is death, no one can die in it. If you say – He experienced death, that means he's still alive. If you can experience birth, you already have to be there before being born – what-you-are. All the re-birth thing is they go back to a point so that they can see that they were already there before the two liquids met. But that didn't help them either because they went to the previous incarnation.

Q [Another visitor]: What is the experience of absence?

K: You have the experience of absence even here when you drink too much. Suddenly there's an absence of the 'me' and there's no time, there's only an empty 'I'. You experience the absence of a 'me'.

Q: But when you die...

K: There's neither experience nor no experience. You cannot make anything out of it. There cannot be an experience of That. How can there be an experience of That? You can experience the absence but not That what is inspite or prior to the experience of absence-presence. When there's no experiencer, how can you experience something? That's deep-deep sleep because there's no experiencer and nothing to experience – and still you are.

So, what-you-are doesn't need any presence of an experiencer. And from there the experiencer experiencing what can be experienced arises. But you don't arise in it. You start dreaming as an experiencer – dreamer dreaming what can be dreamt. But you are already there before the dreaming happens. So, you don't depend on the way you dream.

But now you think you depend on the way you dream to be what-you-are. That by dreaming right, you become That what-you-are. What an idea that you can dream your truth! If I had an interest in bringing people to the silver light, I can just chop their question. But I have no interest. For me it's not better or worse. It just happens sometimes but not because I see an advantage in it. If someone is in golden awareness light – who cares? It's like a running advertisement for *vipassana*. I give a shit about it.

Q [Another visitor]: What is the essence of consciousness?

K: Consciousness.

Q: Substratum?

K: Consciousness. Why do you have to repeat it? Consciousness. It's like what's the essence of Self? Self!

Q: That's true for everything. The nature of fun is fun...

K: Yeah. That's called noumenon. The nature of beauty is beauty, the nature of knowledge is knowledge, the nature of world is world, the nature of a man is man, the nature of a woman is a woman. It's easy. The nature of real is real. The nature of unreal is unreal. You can go on and on. Everything is as it is.

Q [Another visitor]: So, we cannot do anything but we have to do something...

K: You have never done or not done anything. You have never done anything and will never do anything. Things happen by themselves, but nothing ever happened.

Q [Another visitor]: When you say it's stupid, what does that mean?

K: It's like doing as if you don't know.

Q: But isn't it a paradox?

K: No. You have to play stupid otherwise you cannot experience anything. It's not a paradox, it's just a necessity. You have to do as if you have a body. So, you play stupid but after a while, you forget that you play stupid and then you are stupid.

Q: But is that natural?

K: Don't start the vomiting again here.

Q: I can see what that makes you vomit but yet...

K: You are not in a court house. You are not being accused of having done something. You don't have to explain why you are stupid, you are just stupid.

Q: That I like...

K: You don't have to say it's natural.

Q: It's just the way you say it, it sounds bad...

K: It is bad because you suffer about your bloody stupidity. It's stupid to suffer. There's no reason for it. There's nothing coming out of that stupidity or suffering. You always think that when I suffer, there must be some reward afterwards. I would get something out of it. No you just suffer and nothing would come out of it. *Mea-maximum-culpa*.

You think that you suffer but at the end you would see the light. You're just stupid.

Q: Is it personal or impersonal?

K: Doesn't matter. You're just stupid. [Laughter] Just be the stupidity itself but don't be the one who is stupid.

Q: That's the paradox...

K: No. You take it personal.

Q: But to live this, there's a paradox...

K: It's not living it. Living is living the personal moment-by-moment story but in being stupid, there's no time in That, there's no moment-by-moment. But you want to make it moment-by-moment.

Q: So, which one's better?

K: There's only the living dead. You want to be the living dead or stupidity? [Laughter] Stupid living or living stupid. What do you want? You want to stay a virgin and still fuck. You don't want to miss the relative life but you also want That what-you-are. You want both. You are afraid that you would miss something in the relative. You want That but you don't want to give up this – that's stupid.

You cannot just play relative and think that you can just play it. You will be sucked in again – if you like it or not. Then you suffer again. You are what-you-are – final. It's not being half here and half there. That's your fear. You fear that you will miss something here but you are longing for That. That's stupid. But you cannot decide.

Okay. Go, but really go. [Clapping]

October 7, 2012. Evening Talk.
Mallorca, Spain

www.ingramcontent.com/pod-product-compliance
Lightning Source LLC
Chambersburg PA
CBHW070646160426
43194CB00009B/1602